THE BOURNE SOCIETY

Village Histories

5. COULSDON

Editor: Ian Scales

Series Editors: Roger Packham and Gwyneth Fookes

ISBN 0 900992 50 6

Acknowledgements

A large number of people have contributed to the production of the fifth volume of the Village History Series. Not only the authors of the various chapters, but each of them will no doubt have called on their spouses, partners, friends and neighbours for assistance in their efforts to get to the bottom of all the queries that inevitably occur in the gathering together of such a large amount of information. Life would have been much more difficult, too, if it were not for the enthusiasm of numerous librarians and museum staff. We appreciate their help.

We greatly appreciate the help that Mrs Lucy Butler gave us in making accessible a number of photographs of the Byron family.

Roger Packham has, as always, kindly loaned a number of photographs from his invaluable collection.

Robert Warner's expertise in desk-top publishing is much appreciated. Use of modern computer technology enables us to produce 'camera ready' copy 'in house' for the printers, giving us control over typesetting and with considerable cost advantages.

Without the help of so many people, this book would not have seen the light of day. Thank you all.

Cover photograph by Andrew Scott
The pond on Bradmore Green in Springtime 2000

CONTENTS

Illustrations

Chapter 6 – Victorian Coulsdon

Chapter 7 - The Byrons of Coulsdon

Chapter 8 – World War I

Chapter 9 – Urban Development between the Wars

Chapter 10 – Reminiscences

Chapter 11 – World War II

Chapter 12 – From 1945 to the Millennium

Chapter 13 - Churches and Chapels

Chapter 14 – Public Transport and Communications

Chapter 15 – Farming and Farms from the mid 19th Century

Chapter 16 – Public Services and Industry in Coulsdon

Chapter 20 – Open Spaces and Countryside

Chapter 21 – Personalities

VIII

Introduction

The Bourne Society is delighted with the success of the *Village Histories* series. It has been most gratifying to see members of the Society and of the public at large reaching for a copy of the appropriate volume to use as a reference work and to check on some detail.

On embarking on *Volume 5: Coulsdon* we were warned that there had already been various historical books published and that 'surely the subject had already been covered in those'. The Bourne Society itself thoroughly researched the area for its *Coulsdon – Downland Village* edited by Una Broadbent and Ronald Latham, now out of print. However, the quantity of new material that our authors have produced is quite remarkable and the number of historical illustrations found has also been impressive. There is enough 'copy' to fill 500 pages, but it is not practical for the Society to produce such a large tome. The same was true for the earlier volumes. Ian Scales and the *Coulsdon* team are to be congratulated on their effort and enthusiasm. The unused material will not be wasted and will hopefully be published elsewhere by the Society.

Coulsdon has impressive – visible – ancient history in the Celtic fields on Farthing Downs high above the Victorian development in Smitham Bottom. Some of the old hilltop farms can still be found, notably Bradmore Farm in its idyllic setting on Bradmore Green in Old Coulsdon. The agriculture based community was for hundreds of years thinly spread out over the hills and valleys which are now occupied by bustling city-orientated commuters.

When the *Village Histories* project was proposed the Coulsdon research team was one of the first to set to work, under the leadership of Commander Mack, but as it was not feasible to publish more than one volume a year, the work slowed down. Sadly Commander Mack did not live to see the finished product, becoming ill and dying in 1996. He wrote the original versions of the earliest chapters and his name has been joined with that of Joy Gadsby in appreciation of his work. Ian Scales took over the reins of editor and has added both serious and light-hearted notes to the researched history.

Village Histories: Coulsdon does not claim to be a definitive history, but we hope that it will stimulate residents' interest in their locality, and that some may be sufficiently enthused by it to themselves become involved in local history. The editors will be very pleased to hear from readers who have information and/or illustrations that give further insight into the people and events recorded in this book.

Gwyneth Fookes

Roger Packham

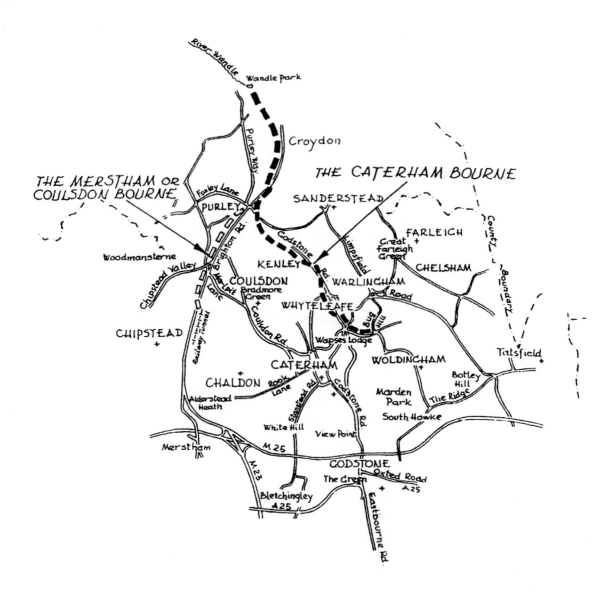

The Bourne Society Area

Chapter 1

Chronology

by Ian Scales

c. 100,000 BC   Mammoths and hippopotami roamed in the region; fossils found in 1897

Tooth of a Mammoth *Elephas primigenius* found near Coulsdon on 20 January 1897 40 feet down in a railway cutting.

Now in the Horniman Museum, London.

Photo: Gwyneth Fookes

c. 100,000 BC	Evidence of early man from the discovery of flint hand-axes.
c. 2000 BC	Bronze age – the first smiths arrived. A metal worker's hoard of bronze has been found in Mead Way.
c. 550 BC	Probable date of Celtic field system on Farthing Downs.
AD 100	Construction of Roman road across Riddlesdown.
c. AD 300	Other evidence of Roman occupation in the area – a burial site was found in Coulsdon Woods Estate in 1969.
c. 648	Probable date of the burial mounds on Farthing Downs of Saxon origin with grave contents. Perhaps one of the incumbents is Cuthraed, a Saxon chief, from whom possibly the name Coulsdon is derived.
675	Probable date of grant of **Coulsdon** manor to Chertsey Abbey by Surrey sub-king Frithwald.
727	Alternative date for above charter to Chertsey Abbey.
1086	Colesdone recorded in Domesday Book – with a church and an approximate population of 45-60. Parts of the present church date from Anglo-Saxon times.
12th century	Break-up of **Watendone** manor & formation of **Garston** manor during Henry III's reign.
1191	**Taunton** sub-manor formed at the end of the 3rd Crusade.

1202	Freehold of sub-manor of **Hooley** granted to Roger de Holegh. It comprised one hide (120 acres).
1234	Margaret of **Taunton** granted a 'cell' to the master and brethren of the Knights Hospitaller of the Order of St Thomas of Acre. The gift included land near St John's church together with messuages and the men to work the land (**Taunton Farm**).

Arms of the Knights of St Thomas of Acre on a roof-rib at Taunton Manor. The hall was subsequently floored at the spring of the arch.

Photograph courtesy of Purley Library

1258	Thomas de Holegh, son of Roger, relinquished **Hooley** to Robert de Waleton.
1260	Robert de Waletone was granted **'our Court at Cullesdone'** next to St John's church.
1266	Robert de la Wode of **Coulsdon** murdered Ralph de Kackeboye.
1268-9	Joel de la Garston conveyed the house and 120 acres at **Garston** to Roger de Horne for 80 marks (£53.6s.8d).
1290	Some of the lands granted to **Taunton** were alienated, with further disputes over the following 100 years on rent to Chertsey Abbey.
1300	Charter gave freehold of estate to Purlee family in **Standene** at 10s.0d p.a. rent.
1312	John de Wood of **Wood Place** died. As an idiot, his lands passed to the Crown (Edward II), but were later restored to Lucy de Wood.
1323	Peter and Julyan de Pirlee had a licence for a chapel at **Hooley** estate from Bishop of Winchester.

CHRONOLOGY

1333	Thomas de Purle acquired land and tenements from Henry de Lacy who had held them for Abbot John de Rutherwyke at a rent of 6s.8d; these were in the area of **Lacey Green**.
1341-2	Dispute with the Knights at **Taunton** concerning a gate and illegal enclosure of the abbot's land; the latter led to John de Redels of Riddlesdown, tenant of Taunton, paying an extra ½d p.a. rent.
1345	William de Holegh died.
1349	**The Black Death.** The population of England was 4 to 5 million before this. See note 1450.
1357	Peter atte Wood had a licence from the Bishop of Winchester for an oratory at **Hooley**.
1362	John Pertenhale & Thomas Gerlethorpe (Rector of Coulsdon) named as holders of **Portnalls** sub-manor.
1373	Abbot John Uske granted land in Kenley to Peter and Laurentia atte Wood of **Wood Place**. On Peter's death the lands passed to his son-in-law Hugh Quecche, who held the lands on behalf of his wife Elizabeth (née atte Wood).
1385	Coulsdon & Woodmansterne Rector John Felett was accused of poaching with others on **Hartley Warren.**
1391	Nicholas Carew had bought **Hooley** from John de Purlee and was reported for neglecting repairs to the King's highway at a place called Popildelane; the entire parish of **Coulsdon** was held responsible for the resulting floods.
1395	A stile at **Lacies** was defiled by John Godman, who was fined 3d.
1398	**Tollers** Farmhouse was burnt down; William Toller was ordered to rebuild it. Charles Colgryme was suspected of arson.
1403	Hugh Quecche of **Wood Place** died. His heiress was daughter Joan, Peter and Laurentia's granddaughter (see 1373).
1412	Thomas de Purlee failed to keep the King's highway clear by not tree lopping at **Collysdon Strete.**
1415	Geoffrey de Lacey granted the right to farm **Hartleys** as well as **Laceys**. He built a house at Hartleys.
1430	Both Thomas de Purlee and his son John died.
1438-42	Dispute over an oak tree between John Pertenhale of **Portnalls** and Richard Lane who held **Hooley.**
1442	John Pertenhale conveyed **Portnalls** sub-manor to Richard Rokenham.
1443	The Court Rolls record trouble with Abbot of Chertsey concerning lands at **Wood Place**, now held by Richard Colcoke who also had a deed for lands called **Pirle in Coulsdon**.
1446	Richard Colcoke of **Wood Place** was at court for brewing ale and was fined 2d.
1450	Four **Coulsdon** yeomen (Thos Basset snr & jnr, John Basset and Richard Rokenham) pardoned after Jack Cade's rising in Kent. 'All other men of the vill' were included in the pardon.
Note:	The population of England had never recovered from the Black Death 100 years earlier. It was estimated at this time still to be only about 2¼ million – half of what it had been.

1490	John Attwood was assessed for 3 days service to be paid to King Henry VII, for three holdings in **Coulsdon.**
1496	The **Hooley** indenture was mentioned as having belonged formerly to John Pays.
1523	**Hooley** let to John Lamberd by indenture under seal of Abbot of Chertsey.
1536	**Dissolution of Monastery of Chertsey**.
1537	The Hospital of St Thomas at **Taunton** was suppressed and sold. The full annual rent of possessions totalled 100s.
1537	Sir Nicholas Carew acquired freehold of **Coulsdon** manor.
1538	Sir Nicholas Carew executed and **Coulsdon** manor transferred to the Crown.
1539	Lady Malin Carew, Sir Nicholas' mother, rented **Portnalls.**
1554	Sir Francis Carew was granted the manor of **Coulsdon,** including **Hooley** sub-manor, by Queen Mary.
1589	Legal transfer of lordship of **Coulsdon Manor** from Carew to Darcy, which took effect in 1611 on the death of Sir Francis Carew.
1631	The monument to Grace Rowed installed in St John's church.
1664	25 of 31 listed Coulsdon householders eligible for payment of **Hearth Tax.**
1675	A peal of five bells was cast for St John's church. They are still in regular use.
1680	*The Red Lion* is shown on John Seller's map.

One of the earliest known photographs of the original *Red Lion*, Smitham Bottom. *c.*1905

1731	First mention of cricket being played in Smitham Bottom.
1760	First reference to a windmill on Coulsdon Common, where Windmill House now stands. It was demolished in 1880.

CHRONOLOGY

1760 — The folly of seven beech trees on **Farthing Downs** was planted on the instructions of Thomas Harley of Hooley House. (He was later Lord Mayor of London). Only one original tree remains, the others having been replaced during the 1990s.

1762 — **Place House Farm** with over 170 acres belonged to Thomas Winch.

1762 — The Messeder map was produced.

Hartley Farm

as shown in Messeder's Field Book

1762

Courtesy of Purley Library

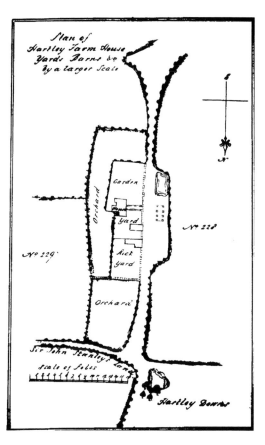

1777 — A second windmill was built on Coulsdon Common. It was demolished in 1924.

1782 — **Thomas Byron** purchased Coulsdon Manor.

1785 — **Bainbridge map** of Coulsdon was produced.

1788 — The **Prince of Wales** watched a bare-knuckle fight at *The Red Lion*.

1801 — **Thomas Byron** moved to Hooley House, becoming Coulsdon's first resident squire. He died there in 1821.

1805 — The **Croydon, Merstham & Godstone Railway** (CM&GR) was built through Coulsdon. It was the first public railway in the world.

1808 — **The Foxley Hatch** (Purley) to **Reigate** toll road opened. The tolls were abolished in 1865.

1824 — **Hall & Co** was founded, largely on the business of transporting Merstham firestone and lime by way of the CM&GR, for rebuilding London Bridge.

1838	Extensive purchase of land by the **London & Brighton Railway Company** resulted in the CM&GR being closed and Squire Byron having to move from Hooley House to **Portnalls Farm.**
1841	The **London to Brighton railway** was opened. **Stoats Nest Station** was opened, but was closed again for passenger traffic in 1856.
1850	**Hartley Farm** demolished and **Coulsdon Court** built on the site for Byron.
1864	**Marlpit Lane Quarry** commenced work; owned by Hall & Co.
c.1869	The Caterham Spring Water Co began to supply some Coulsdon properties with **water.**
1871	Wickham Flower carried out archaeological excavations on **Farthing Downs.**
1878	**Cane Hill** Asylum commenced on 148 acres of land purchased for £23,000 from Joseph Tucker, being part of Portnalls Farm. It was opened in 1883 with 1,100 patients and expanded in 1888 to 2000 patients.
1883	The Lord Mayor of London formally dedicated the commons of Coulsdon, Kenley, Farthing Downs & Riddlesdown as open spaces in perpetuity.
1889	**Coulsdon South** railway station opened, mainly to serve Cane Hill Asylum.
1891	**Coppard's Temperance Hotel** was opened on the corner of Brighton Road and Lion Green Road. It was closed in 1934.
1899	A new **Stoats Nest Station** opened, half a mile south of its predecessor.
1901	**Fanfare Road**, commenced, named for the coronation of King Edward VII. It was later renamed **Downs Road.**
1904	**Smitham Station** was opened, giving Coulsdon its third railway station.
1905	The first London to Brighton motor bus started service along Brighton Road.
1910	Railway crash at **Stoats Nest Station.** 7 killed, 42 injured.
1911	**Stoats Nest Station** renamed as a result of the crash, becoming **Coulsdon West** and later **Coulsdon North.**
1911	**Methodist Church,** Brighton Road, opened.
1912	**Hooley House** was sold and became **Ashdown Park Hotel,** with golf course and bowling greens.
1913	The first sod for the present **St Andrew's Church** was cut.
1915	**Coulsdon & Purley Urban District Council** was formed.
1916	Original **St Aidan's Church** built in Woodcote Grove Road, now a Martial Arts Centre.
1919	**The Comrades Club** for survivors of World War I was opened in Brighton Road.
1920	**Coulsdon Memorial Recreation Ground** was opened in Marlpit Lane.
1921	**Edmund Byron**, the last resident squire of Coulsdon Manor, died aged 77.
1922	**Byron land** sold for development, resulting in great expansion of the population.
1923	**Electric trains** replaced steam trains to Coulsdon.
1928	**Coulsdon North locomotive depôt** was closed.

CHRONOLOGY

1928	*The Red Lion* was rebuilt.
1933	New **Comrades Club** building on Brighton Road site was opened by Admiral Goodenough.
c. 1933	**Tudor estate** and shops commenced.
1933	**Purley High School for Boys, now Coulsdon College,** moved from Purley to Placehouse Lane.
1936	Coulsdon **Library** in Brighton Road was opened.
1939	**Purley Grammar School for Girls** moved from Purley to Stoneyfield Road.
1940	**Coulsdon** was bombed for the first time and St John's Church was damaged.
1944	**V1** flying bombs ('Doodlebugs'), falling short of London, struck Coulsdon.
1948	Brian Hope-Taylor excavated burial mounds on **Farthing Downs.**
1959	A 350-seat extension to **St John's Church** was opened.
1961	The **Ashdown Park Hotel** closed – it was demolished in 1971; the site is now a housing estate.
1963	**Bradmore Green Library** was opened.
1964	The present **St Aidan's** Church was built.
1964	**Coulsdon & Purley Urban District Council** ceased to exist when the district was absorbed into the London Borough of Croydon.
1975	**1,300 years of Coulsdon were commemorated**; since the Abbot of Chertsey Abbey was appointed Lord of the Manor in AD 675.
1984	**Coulsdon North** station closed.
1988	Closure of Purley County Grammar School for Boys, to be succeeded by **Purley Sixth Form College.**
1992	**Cane Hill Hospital** closed

SOURCES

Bourne Society **Bulletins** & *Local History Records*

BROADBENT, U & LATHAM, R (Eds) (1976) *Coulsdon – Downland Village,* Bourne Society

Coulsdon Library

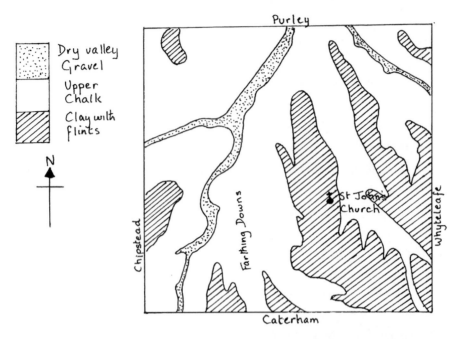

Sketch plan showing the geology of the area

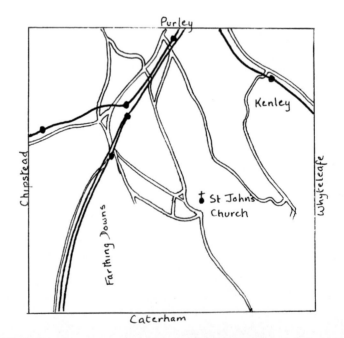

Sketch plan showing how development followed the lines of the valleys

Chapter 2

Beginnings – From Prehistory to Roman Times

by Joy Gadsby

(with contributions from Robert Mack)

Coulsdon is situated on a promontary of high ground jutting northwards from the ridge of the North Downs. Further north it includes the valley of Smitham Bottom and originally also included the lower lying areas which are now part of Kenley and Purley. Through this valley the Coulsdon bourne flowed, meeting another stream coming from Kingswood at Smitham Bottom, and the Caterham bourne at Purley. The three united bournes join the Wandle at Croydon and thence flow to the Thames at Wandsworth and the sea. Today the Bourne mostly flows underground, only surfacing at times of exceptionally wet weather – rarely now causing flooding in Marlpit Lane, at Whyteleafe and Purley. These were the so-called 'woe waters' said to predict catastrophe.

The underlying rock is chalk; over which on the high ground lies a layer of clay-with-flints of varying thickness. Although the chalk is pervious, producing a warm thin dry soil, the presence of clay enables water to be ponded, and the ready supply of flints made it a very suitable area for early man to survive.

The earliest evidence we have of human habitation in Coulsdon is from the Old Stone Age, some 100,000 years ago – known as the ***Palaeolithic***. These people left behind their beautifully 'tooled' hand-axes, including one at Chaldon (TQ 325552) and another in Coulsdon (TQ 298587). In these pre-glacial times elephant, rhinoceros and hippopotamus were among the animals that were hunted, and proof of their presence was found at Cane Hill in 1897. The early inhabitants either died out or retreated further south as each successive ice-age swept down from the north, the last one of which reached North London about 10,000 years ago.

Once the ice began to melt a new invasion over the land which at that time joined Britain to the continent took place, and people of the Middle Stone Age – or ***Mesolithic*** – once more roamed over the south-east. They were a nomadic people, living by hunting, fishing and gathering wild plants and fruits. Although most of the area would have been forested at that time, there is evidence that the first clearings were made, where animals would come to feed and drink, and where they could be more easily caught. Among the animals they hunted would have been bears and wolves, as well as many of the mammals more familiar to us today. It is possible that they also began herding animals, especially deer. These *Mesolithic* peoples were the first dog trainers, using domesticated dogs to help them hunt. They had also discovered, by trial and error, which plants were edible.

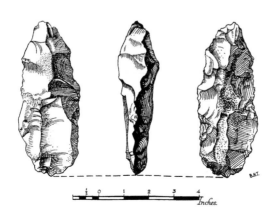

Stone Age flint axe found on Farthing Downs by Brian Hope-Taylor

Surrey Archaeological Collections XLIX (1946)

By about 4000 BC important social and economic changes were on the way. The discovery that certain grasses could be made to yield a nutritious food source, and that they could be improved, enabled people to settle in one place and to work the land. The first farmers – *Neolithic* men – had arrived. Flint was still the main material used for weapons and tools, either alone or hafted into wood, and wood was very much used in ***neolithic*** times for building dwellings, fencing settlements,

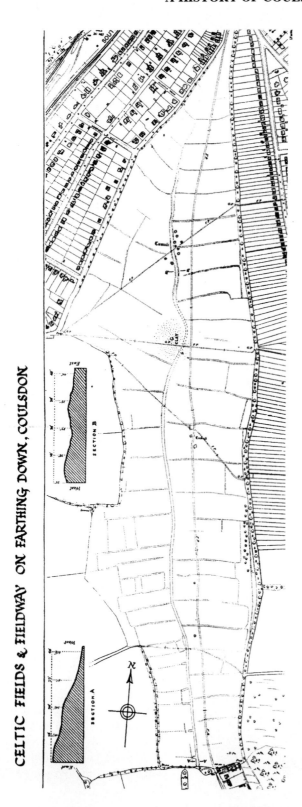

CELTIC FIELDS & FIELDWAY ON FARTHING DOWN, COULSDON

Celtic fields and fieldway on Farthing Downs

Surrey Archaeological Collections **L** (1947)

Courtesy of Surrey Archaeological Society

making tools, including ploughs or 'ards', and also weaving looms – there is evidence that these people could spin and weave. Wool from their sheep and goats, linen and hemp from their crops, were used in clothing as were animal skins, which had been the main 'textiles' available to their predecessors. The extensive use of wood, together with the slash-and-burn technique used to clear the ground for crops, resulted in the forest cover being very much reduced, and the landscape became a very different one from that found by the first inhabitants of Coulsdon.

With the discovery of metal-working even greater changes occurred. There is no real divide between the late Neolithic and the early metal ages – gold, silver, copper and tin being the earliest metals used. For some time the two cultures existed side by side, but the discovery of bronze – an alloy of copper and tin – brought with it considerable changes. There was in fact an 'industrial revolution' as important as that of the 18th and 19th centuries, if not more so.

With bronze-working, many – more sophisticated – artifacts became available and considerable trade developed with continental Europe. The 'common market' is nothing new! In Mead Way, Coulsdon a hoard of bronze was found at what appeared to be the site of a metal-worker's workshop (TQ 306581), and other evidence of bronze-working was found at Woodcote (TQ 297615). As those with knowledge of how to mine, smelt and work metals grew increasingly important, the acquisition of wealth by the few over the many gave rise to a more hierarchical society.

Bronze was followed by the discovery of iron – a metal much more widely available and very plentiful in the south-east of England. It was in the **Iron Age** that Coulsdon began to be truly 'on the map'. Gradually spreading from eastern Europe to the west from about 550 BC, the Iron Age or Celtic people brought with them a higher standard of living, better tools and enhanced artistic development. There is evidence of their presence on Farthing Downs, where an extensive Celtic field system can still be seen. Their fields were rectangular in shape

One of the many Celtic field boundary banks on Farthing Downs, with Saxon tumuli on the skyline
Courtesy Corporation of London/ A Scott

and divided by earth banks. As you walk or drive up the main track across the downs you pass over some of these earth banks. They are not, as might be supposed, 'sleeping policemen for traffic calming' but the vestiges of those Celtic earth banks, extending across the downs to each side of the track, best seen in the low sun on a winter's afternoon. Further evidence of Celtic fields can be found on the west side of the downs, towards Woodplace Farm and Netherne Lane, and also at Coulsdon Court.

Farming in Iron Age Britain was well developed – at least ten cereal crops were grown as well as peas, beans and other legumes; cattle, pigs, sheep and goats were reared, and rotation of crops and dunging of fields practised. Woodland management was also well advanced, with coppicing used to produce timbers for dwellings and for stockades to protect cattle etc.

The **Romans** invaded and settled in Britain in AD 43 but the evidence for their presence in Coulsdon is tantalisingly small. Antiquarians of the 17th and 18th centuries maintained that there was a Roman town at nearby Woodcote, but extensive building development in the 19th and early 20th centuries seems to have wiped out all the evidence. Romano-British pottery has been found at several sites in Coulsdon, including Marlpit Lane Quarry, Netherne, and on Farthing Downs. A Roman burial site was found in June 1969 at Coulsdon Woods (TQ 302595) and the Roman Road from London to Portslade crossed the slopes of Riddlesdown and on through Caterham, so there is every reason to believe that the Romans made their presence felt in Coulsdon.

A Roman coin – an AE4 of Constantius II – and coffin nails found in one of the Romano-British burials in 1969

The Celtic peoples certainly adopted many Roman customs, but the Romans also acquired much from the Celts. They were particularly intrigued by the clothes they wore – the trousers, which the Romans called *Bracchii* (from which we get our word 'breeches') and the woollen cloaks worn by the Celts. These were much prized and the Romans called them the *Birrus Britannicus* and exported them to other parts of the Roman Empire. Is it too fanciful to suggest that some of these cloaks may have been woven in Coulsdon? Certainly the 'Made in Britain' label has a long pedigree!

Despite the length of time – nearly 400 years – that the Romans occupied Britain, the legacy of their presence locally is small and it is to the succeeding invaders, the Anglo-Saxons, that Coulsdon owes its name and its earliest documented foundation.

SOURCES

Anglo-Saxon Chronicle trans. Garmonsway G N, 2nd edition, London 1972

CUNLIFFE, B *Iron Age Britain*. English Heritage (English Historical Documents, No. 97, 2nd Edition)

FARLEY, M (1967) *Guide to Antiquities* Bourne Society

LAING, L & LAING, J (1980) *The Origins of Britain*, Paladin

Chapter 3

Before The Norman Conquest

by Joy Gadsby

The Romans officially abandoned Britain in AD 410 but the Anglo-Saxons had already begun to threaten invasion, in answer to which the Romans had established the 'forts of the Saxon Shore' facing those areas of the European mainland from which the main threat came. Eventually they did come, not in great hordes but in smaller groups, settling down and driving the Romano-British Celts further and further west.

Saxon grave found during archaeological excavations on Farthing Downs by Brian Hope-Taylor 1948

Courtesy Hulton-Deutsch Collection Ltd

In the south-east they gained an early foothold; Saxon settlements from the 7th and 8th centuries AD have been found in Croydon, Mitcham, Beddington and Bromley, and there is evidence to suggest that they also settled in Coulsdon at about this period. Nearly all the names for the villages within the Bourne Society's area are of Saxon origin – for example Chipstead, Chaldon, Warlingham – and Coulsdon is no exception. The pronunciation and spelling of Coulsdon has varied down the ages, but appeared first as Cuthredesdone in Anglo-Saxon times. Tradition says that Cuthraed was a Saxon chief, and it has been claimed that he was the son of Cenwalh, the King of the West Saxons. It was he who in AD 648 was given, according to *The Anglo-Saxon Chronicle,* 'three thousand hides of land by Ashdown'. A sub-manor of Coulsdon did have the name Ashdown for a time, but it is more likely that the Ashdown spoken of in the *Chronicle* was much further west, on the Wiltshire downs where there was a great battle in AD 661. Be that as it may, burial mounds of Saxon origin were found on Farthing Downs, and excavations of the main barrow in 1871 revealed the skeleton of a very tall man, with a sword and a shield boss, both of which are now in the Ashmolean Museum. These finds suggest a man of some importance. Other graves nearby yielded a wooden drinking vessel, with chased and gilded bronze hoops, and a gold medallion. In 1948/49 other skeletons were found with iron knives or 'seaxes' from which the name Saxon is derived. One group of five included a young boy with a miniature spear, and smaller finds included beads, bone and silver pins, a purse-mount, comb and a pair of shears – i.e. domestic goods as well as articles of war. The interment of these persons with grave goods, and the alignment of the graves north/south rather than east/west suggests a pre-Christian date for these burials.

Reconstruction of Anglo-Saxon wooden drinking vessel (stoup) found in a tumulus on Farthing Downs in 1871

The Venerable Bede recorded that at a place called Cerotaesei (modern Chertsey) an English monastery was founded in AD 673 by Erkenwald, who later became Bishop of London. The influence of monasteries such as Chertsey grew, and it became the practice for wealthy landowners to grant them gifts of land. Thus in AD 675, according to a charter held by the Abbey, Frithewald, an under-king of the Surrey Saxons gave to Chertsey land at Banstede, Chepstede-cum-Chalvedoe (Chaldon), Cuthredesdone and Whatendone.

There is some doubt about the validity of this charter and the date of it. In the 10th century, Chertsey Abbey was sacked by the Danes and its papers and deeds lost. It became commonplace to reconstruct these charters, and there were monastic centres that specialised in 're-inventing' them. In a sense they were forgeries, but were probably based on oral tradition and may therefore have been reasonably accurate. Chertsey Abbey was refounded in about AD 964 and reclaimed its former properties including Coulsdon.

What would life in Cuthredesdone have been like? Almost all the domestic buildings in Saxon times were of wood, and little has survived except the holes made by the support posts. It is likely that the inhabitants of Coulsdon in those days lived in little more than huts made of wattle and daub – often flimsy structures, with a central hearth from which the smoke would escape as best it could through a hole in the roof or cracks in the walls. Any windows would have been unglazed, with perhaps a piece of sacking or leather as a blind to keep out the cold and rain. The family would have shared its home with its animals, occupying different ends of the house – a situation that may have been odorous but which would nevertheless have provided a certain amount of warmth.

We know from Domesday Book that when William's great survey was made in 1086 there was a church in Coulsdon, and this may have been of stone, flint or timber, certainly of a more substantial structure than the peasants' housing. The Abbot of Chertsey would also have had a bailiff, looking after the affairs of the abbey, and therefore a more substantial building probably served as a manor house for the abbot's servants.

**The armorial achievement of
Chertsey Abbey**

CHERTSEY ABBEY.
*Party or and argent St.
Paul's sword argent with
its hilt or crossed with
St. Peter's keys gules and
azure.*

Coinage had been introduced before the Romans, but most local trade was by barter and few Coulsdon citizens would have possessed money as such. The community would have been largely self-supporting, its inhabitants tilling the land, keeping livestock to provide them with milk, eggs and bacon, and making use of wild fruits and herbs both for food, medicine, floor coverings and many other uses around the home. Local woods provided building materials, firewood and fencing.

Coulsdon had an open field system, worked by the local people, each one having a number of strips in each of the large fields. Most communities had a three-field system, but Coulsdon seems to have had a four-field one. In addition to working on their own strips, the people would have worked on the 'demesne' land – the portion that was reserved for the Abbey's own use. What was grown in the fields was a community decision – probably rotating barley and other cereals, beans, and fallow. Ploughs and other implements were shared.

The Saxons were good administrators. Long before the coming of Duke William in 1066, they had divided the country into shires, the shires or counties into hundreds and the hundreds into parishes. The parish boundaries remained largely unaltered until the 20th century. Thus when eventually in 1066 William of Normandy defeated the Saxon King Harold at Hastings in Sussex, he found a kingdom that already had a good basis for administration and a fiscal system second to none.

SOURCES

The Anglo Saxon Chronicle, trans. G N Garmonsway, 2nd edn (London 1972)

BIDEN, N, GADSBY, J M & SCALES, I (Ed) (1998) *A brief guide to the Parish Church of St John the Evangelist, Coulsdon*

BROADBENT, U & LATHAM, R (Eds) (1976) *Coulsdon – Downland Village.* The Bourne Society

LAING, L & LAING, J (1982) *Anglo-Saxon England* Paladin

MALDEN, H E (Ed) (1902-12) *Victoria County History of the County of Surrey*

MORRIS, J (Ed) (1975) *Domesday Book – 3. Surrey* Phillimore

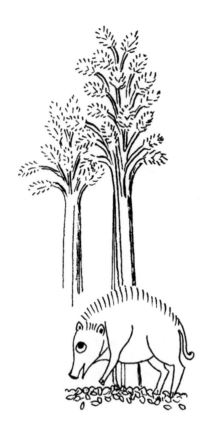

'Woodland for 3 Pigs'

At the time of the Domesday survey Coulsdon villagers had the right to pasture pigs in the local woodland – possibly that still called 'Inwood'

Chapter 4

Domesday Coulsdon

by Joy Gadsby

It is unlikely that there were any immediate fundamental changes in the lives of the inhabitants of Coulsdon, when William became King. He was careful not to change existing Anglo-Saxon laws except where they were in conflict with his rule over his newly gained territory. He established control by putting his supporters into positions of power, leaving those properties that were held by the church in ecclesiastical ownership, but replacing the Saxon hierarchy with his own Norman monks and bishops.

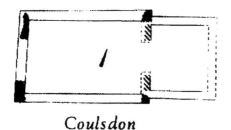

Coulsdon

Plan of the original Saxon church at Coulsdon, based on the *Victoria County History*, showing the fragmentary remains that exist within the present structure

At Christmas in 1085, King William held court at Gloucester and calling together all his councillors ordered that a survey should be made of how much land there was in each shire, how much was in the hands of the king himself, how much livestock there was, what dues he received each year from the shires, how much land his archbishops, diocesan bishops, abbots and earls had, and how much money it was worth. This was to be done within a year and the results brought back to him the following Christmas. That it was possible for this to be done was largely due to the sound administrative structure inherited from the Saxons.

Imagine the excitement, confusion, fear and suspicion that the survey must have caused. In fact the word Domesday *(Doomsday)* was coined by the populace because once the facts were written down there was no appeal against them. William's teams of investigators (he sent out two teams, the second one to check up on the findings of the first!) spoke Norman French, but the inhabitants of the villages spoke Anglo-Saxon. Small wonder then that anomalies occurred in the records, some items obviously omitted and some meanings obscure.

The survey for Coulsdon translates as follows—

> 'The Abbey of St Peter of Chertsey holds Colesdone. In King Edward's time it was assessed at 10 hides, now 3½. There is land for 10 ploughs. In the demesne there is 1 ploughland. There are 10 villeins and 4 cottars with 6 ploughs. There is a church. There is woodland for 3 pigs. In King Edward's time it was worth £6, now £7.'

A 'hide' was originally 120 acres, but by William's time it had come to be interpreted more as a tax unit rather than an accurate land measurement. The 'ploughs' represent 'plough-teams', usually of eight oxen; the 'demesne' was that part of the manor reserved for the lord of the manor and his household, in this case the Abbot of Chertsey.

The 10 villeins represented 10 households, and the cottars likewise represented households, lower down the social scale, renting just a small piece of land for their immediate use, and working as labourers. On an estimated average of between three or four members per family, this gives a population for Coulsdon of around 45-60, excluding the Abbot's own servants living on the estate.

Woodland at three pigs represents an area of woodland for which three pigs were paid to the lord of the manor in respect of the right to pasture the pigs in the woodland, particularly in the autumn, to feed on acorns and beechmast. The levy in Surrey varied from one pig for every seven pastured, to one pig for every 10, but attempts to arrive at the size of woodlands in Domesday Book from the number of pigs pastured have so far failed to provide a satisfactory answer. Note that the land is valued higher now than in King Edward the Confessor's time, reflecting increased values after a period of relative peace.

With the arrival of the Normans came the feudal system of government. Under this the King owned all the land, and the courtiers to whom he had granted land, of whom the Abbot of Chertsey was one, were his tenants-in-chief. These in turn could sub-lease land to appointees approved by the King. The villagers, or villeins, held their lands under the lord of the manor, in return for which they gave service on the demesne lands, and paid certain 'taxes' in kind for various privileges. They were not free to marry without permission or to leave the manor, and were in many ways much less free than they had been under Saxon rule.

Nevertheless the lord of the manor could not go against the 'Custom of the Manor', and every villein had the right – or rather the duty – to attend the manor court and share in decisons that affected the community — what crops should be sown, disputes resolved, and so on. Life was harsh, and in times of bad harvests there was considerable hardship. Working hours were long and leisure time sparse. Nevertheless compared with life in 20th century Britain, there was comfort in shared experience and community support.

At the time of Domesday Book both the manor of 'Colesdone' and also that of neighbouring 'Watendone' are recorded as having a church, and Watendone manor appears to have been larger than 'Colesdone'. Both are assessed at 20 hides in the time of Edward the Confessor, but Watendone had '17 villeins and 2 cottars' compared to Colesdone's '10 villeins and 4 cottars.' Not a great deal is known of the church at Watendone but it never had parochial status. The last known reference to it is in the will of Thomas Bassett from about 1465, which gives its dedication as St Mary the Virgin, after which it seems to have been used as a barn until burnt down in the 18th century. Excavations by The Bourne Society in 1966 revealed the site of the church at Wheat Knoll, east of Hayes Lane, overlooking the Kenley valley, with the hamlet clustered around it. Today, what was once a thriving little community has disappeared, commemorated only by a road name, *The Wattenden Arms* public house and the name of a local school.

Location of the Bourne Society's Watendone excavation 1966

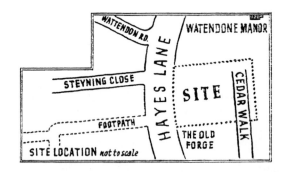

SOURCES

The Anglo Saxon Chronicle trans. G N Garmonsway, 2nd edn (London 1972)

BROADBENT, U & LATHAM R (Eds) (1976) *Coulsdon – Downland Village*. The Bourne Society

MORRIS, J (Ed) (1975) *Domesday Book – Surrey* Phillimore

Chapter 5

A RURAL IDYLL?

From the Middle Ages to the Industrial Revolution

by Joy Gadsby

The Saxon church at Coulsdon was largely replaced in about 1260 by a new building constructed mainly from Merstham firestone – a calcareous sandstone quarried locally. The building was probably overseen by the masons of Chertsey Abbey, and the sedilia and piscina have survived and are considered among the finest examples of the period in England. Adjoining the church was the 'Abbot's Court' or manor house, where the abbot's bailiff lived, and where his steward would have stayed when presiding over meetings of the manor court.

The 13th century piscina and sedilia in St John's Church, Coulsdon

Earlier, at the end of the 12th and early 13th centuries, probably at a time when the population was increasing, several 'sub-manors' were leased out, among them Taunton (1191), Hooley (1202) and Garston (c.1230). Another was the sub-manor of Portnalls, referred to in the manorial records at least from 1362. This increase in the population was reversed at the time of the Black Death in 1349, but the exact effect of this terrible plague on Coulsdon is not known. Overall about one-third of the population of England is estimated to have died.

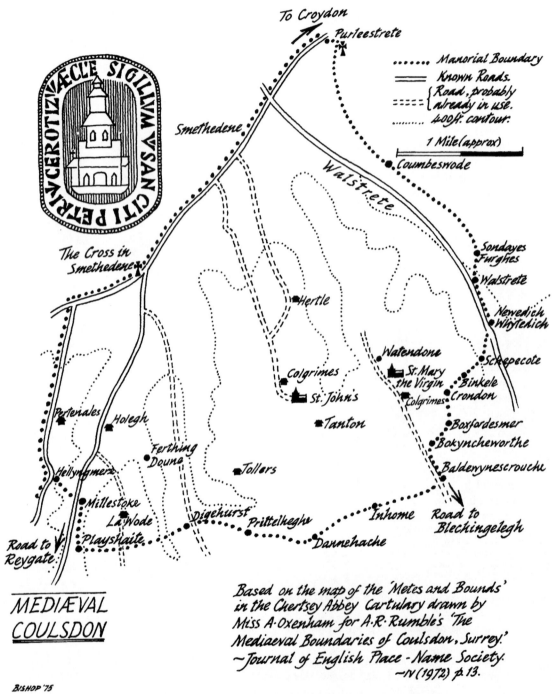

MEDIÆVAL COULSDON

Based on the map of the 'Metes and Bounds' in the Chertsey Abbey Cartulary drawn by Miss A. Oxenham for A. R. Rumble's 'The Mediaeval Boundaries of Coulsdon, Surrey.' ~ Journal of English Place - Name Society. ~ IV (1972) p. 13.

BISHOP '75

A RURAL IDYLL? – FROM THE MIDDLE AGES TO THE INDUSTRIAL REVOLUTION

Taunton Manor was granted in 1235 to the Order of St Thomas the Martyr. The gift was disputed, but in 1260 the Canons who had founded St Thomas's Hospital in London were also confirmed as tenants of Chertsey Abbey and held Taunton Manor until the Dissolution of the Monasteries in 1536. It is thought that part of the original manor house is incorporated in the structure of the present day Taunton Farm. In a survey of 1547 there is mention of a chapel and a hall, and part of the latter can be seen in an upstairs corridor of the farmhouse, with a Maltese Cross, the badge of the order, carved on a roof rib.

The boundaries of the Manor of Coulsdon as described in the Chertsey cartulary read:

'Metes and bounds of Colesdone, namely beginning at Purleestrete beside Smethedene on the east side, and so as far as the wood called Coumbeswode, and so as far as Sondayesfurghes (i.e.Sunday's Furrows) in the heath over against Warlingham; and so it descends by the said heath into the valley as far as the king's highway that leads towards Golstone called Walstrete, and so by the said highway as far as the ditch called le Newedich or Whytedich, and so by that ditch as far as the place that is called Schepecote, and so by Binkele as far as the croft called Crondone, and so by the fences and hedges as far as the pit called Boxfordesmere, and so as far as the field called Bokyncheworthe, and so by the king's highway that leads towards Blechingelegh as far as the cross called Baldewynescrouche (i.e. Baldwin's Cross), and so by the fences and hedges as far as the field of Caterham called Inhome, and so across the heath as far as the place called Dannehache, and so by the fences as far as Prittelheghe, and so as far as Digehurst, and so as far as the place that is called Playshaite, and so as far as Millestoke, and so as far as Hellyngmere, and so as far as the king's highway that leads towards Reygate, and so by that highway as far as the cross in Smethedene, and so in Smethedene by the king's highway that leads towards Croydone as far as Purleestrete aforesaid.'

— and these boundaries can largely still be recognised and followed today.

There have been some colourful inhabitants of Coulsdon from this period, among them Margaret de Passele, who was implicated in the murder of her husband Edward shortly after he had made a will in favour of herself and her sons by a previous marriage. A fortnight after Edward's murder, his 13 year old son, Edmund, by another woman, was murdered in Coulsdon by assassins hired by Margaret. The King ordered their arrest, and that of Margaret, but the accused could not be found. Later that year one of the assassins was caught and tried but acquitted by a Coulsdon jury, as was Margaret herself and a second assassin two years later. Bribery and corruption almost certainly played a part in their acquittal.

Another colourful family was the Colgrimes, whose name suggests they were originally charcoal burners. We first hear of them in a tax return of 1332, when Alice and Robert, villein tenants of the Abbey of Chertsey, were each assessed for tax at 9½d. The Colgrimes seem to have been a quarrelsome family, involved in disputes over land ownership, which land eventually passed in 1339 to the Robert mentioned above.

In the years following the Peasants' Revolt of 1381 other members of the family are prominent. Charles Colgrime was convicted of selling ale by false measure, enclosing a patch of communal land for his own use, and poaching on the Lord of the Manor's land with a ferret. His brother Walter was charged with killing a neighbour's sow and keeping a boar (strictly the prerogative of the Lord of the Manor). His nephew John fled the manor twice, only to be brought back each time and fined. At his third attempt in 1430 he fled into Kent and managed to avoid recapture. John's sister Alice had also fled the manor and was living with Richard Aleyn in Chaldon. Repeated efforts to bring her back failed, and she finally eluded her manorial ties by marrying, not Richard Aleyn but John Tiler of Westerham.

In 1450 Thomas Bassett, another Coulsdon resident, joined Jack Cade's rebellion, together with two of his brothers and John Ruckenham. The last was constable of Wallington Hundred at the time, and Rickman Hill is named after him. Fortunately for them, all four were pardoned for their part in the rebellion. The Wood family was another well-known family – for many years the commonest name in Coulsdon. They farmed at Wood Place and were related to the Atwoods of Sanderstead. Woodplace Farm and Woodplace Lane recall the family.

In 1536, at the Dissolution of the Monasteries under Henry VIII, the Abbey of Chertsey was disbanded and the freehold of the Manor of Coulsdon granted to Sir Nicholas Carew, a favourite of the King. Alas, he did not remain in favour for long and was executed on Tower Hill for treason in 1538. It is significant that in his death-speech, Nicholas Carew recommended to his onlookers that they read the Bible. That he himself was able to read the scriptures and commend the crowd to do so was possible because of the Reformation, and the recent translation of the Bible by Miles Coverdale.

In the same year – 1538 – the Manor of Taunton was transferred to the crown.

The connection of the Carews with Coulsdon dated back at least as far as 1361, and in 1554 the family regained possession of the manor when it was granted by Mary Tudor to Sir Francis Carew of Beddington. With it was included the sub-manor of Hooley. Sir Francis was something of an absentee landlord, preferring to live at Beddington, where he is reputed to have grown the first potatoes to be seen in England, brought over from America by his nephew Sir Walter Raleigh, and where he also built an orangery stocked again with seed brought over from Virginia. He also grew cherries, delaying their ripening so that they were ready for Queen Elizabeth I whom he frequently entertained at Beddington. Sir Francis never married and on his death in 1611 the Manor of Coulsdon passed to his nephew Sir Edward Darcy.

In 1560 the revolt of the catholic Earls of Northumberland and Westmorland in favour of Mary Queen of Scots (known as 'The Pilgrimage of Grace') caused a muster of arms. In default of an army (there was no standing army until Cromwell's time almost a century later) each county was ordered to raise a certain number of soldiers. Coulsdon's quota was three and we know the names — William Stevenes – archer, John Hasewell and Thomas Hethe – pikemen. Coulsdon also supplied weapons — two arquebuses, a pike and a corselet. The Surrey force, under Lord Howard of Effingham, was ordered to be ready to march at an hour's notice, but saw no action.

In 1588 two Coulsdon men served in the camp at Tilbury, mustered against a possible Spanish invasion; their names were Thomas Haswell and Henry Feering. Coulsdon also contributed financially to the campaign against the Spanish Armada, being assessed at £19.7s.0d – a levy of two-fifteenths on the value of goods of each of the 16 householders eligible to pay the tax.

During the Civil War and the Commonwealth (1642-1660) very little of note is recorded as happening in Coulsdon. It was probably a supporter of the Parliamentary cause, since an enquiry in 1655 found no suspected royalists there, and the parish seems to have kept out of the fray and to have concentrated on farming the land in the age-old manner.

St John's parish church had two puritan parish priests about the time of the Civil War. The first, Thomas Gauge, was the incumbent from 1640-1641; he later became the vicar of St Sepulchre's, Holborn, where, despite his puritan leanings, he signed a petition against the execution of Charles I. After the Restoration of Charles II he was removed from office as a nonconformist and retired to Wales, where he translated the Bible and other religious works into Welsh. His successor Richard Roberts was one of the officials appointed during the Commonwealth to examine the fitness of clergy for their position. He too was forced to resign at the Restoration of the Monarchy.

In 1662, in an attempt to restore the solvency of the Crown, Charles II raised a Hearth Tax, payable by all householders whose houses were worth more than 20 shillings a year. It was levied at two shillings per annum for every chimney and out of 31 Coulsdon householders listed in 1664, 25 were eligible for payment of the tax. The largest contributor was the Rector, who had 12 hearths, and among the remainder were Taunton Farm, the house now called The Barn at Bradmore Green, and Windmill Cottage on the Common.

A RURAL IDYLL? – FROM THE MIDDLE AGES TO THE INDUSTRIAL REVOLUTION

In 1663 the lordship of the manor passed to the Earl of Portland on the death of Sir Edward Darcy, and in 1670 it was sold to Sir Richard Mason, ending the long connection with the Carew family and its descendants.

The Great Plague of 1665 passed Coulsdon by. The parish registers for that year record only four burials; by comparison Croydon recorded 141 plague deaths and the figures give an indication of the relative isolation of Coulsdon at that time, even though little more than three miles south of Croydon.

The court rolls and the records from the Surrey Quarter Sessions from the mid 17th century onwards give some further insight into day-to-day life in the manor. There were fines for 'blocking the public way', non-compliance with orders, refusal to accept the public office of constable, for allowing the stocks and whipping posts to fall into disrepair. (Does the latter suggest that the villagers had become more law-abiding, or that they managed to avoid being caught? The latter seems more likely given their earlier history!).

In 1688 the lordship of the manor again changed hands, being passed by Sir Richard Mason's widow to Sir Edward des Bouverie, who was of a family of refugees from the Low Countries.

An inventory of the house of Sarah Hills taken after her death in 1766 gives an insight into the furnishing of houses at the time—

..SARAH HILLS, Widow   1766

Extract from — A full and particular inventory of all and singular the goods, chattles and credits of Sarah Hills, late of Coulsdon, widow, by John Moys and Richard Roffey

In the Garrett
Two half-headed sacking bottom bedsteads, one corded ditto with a straw mat, 3 feather beds, 3 bolsters and part of a chest of drawers, bedstead, 6 blankets, 3 old quilts and 2 coverlids

In the Chamber
Two 4-post bedsteads with one set of blue curtains and rods and one set of green ditto. 2 feather beds, 3 bolsters. 1 pillow, a piece of ticking, 4 blankets, 2 coverlids and a chest

In the next Chamber
A bedstead with yellow china furniture, a feather bed, bolster, 2 pillows, a pillow case, a pair of sheets, 3 blankets, a rug, 3 ash chairs, a table, 2 caps and a napkin

In the New Parlour
A wind stove, blower, fender, shovel, tongs and poker; a clock and cover, a large oval table, 1 small ditto, a small ovall wainscot ditto, a mahogany claw ditto, 10 ash wicker bottom chairs, 1 elbow ditto, a looking glass and 4 prints

In the Room over the Kitchen
A bedstead with green chiney furniture, a feather bed, bolster, two pillows, 3 blankets, a quilt, a double mahogany chest of drawers, 3 draw tables, a walnut tree dressing glass with 1 drawer, 3 beech chairs, a corner ditto and pan, a stove, 2 pair of tongs, a brush, a fire pan, a pair of bellows, a fender, a Windsor chair, close stool and pan, a china punchbowl, 2 basons/cracked, 6 cups and saucers, 3 cups, 6 small pictures, a small pair of scales, an ink stand, 11 pewter dishes and 30 pewter plates

In the next Room
A bedstead with linen furniture, a half headed bedstead, 4 feather beds, 2 bolsters, 5 pillows, 6 blankets, 2 field quilts, 2 window curtains and rods, a large couch, a walnut tree chest of drawers, a large chest and a broken glass

In the Dark Room
A churn, two tubs, 2 lanthorns, 3 mahogany teaboards, a hair broom and a chest

In the Kitchen

A pair of Grates, crane hooks and fender, an iron back, a shovel, tongs and poker, 2 brandirons, a Jack Compleat, spits, gridirons, pottage pot hooks, 2 spits, a flesh fork, a pair of stilyards, 2 clevers, a sifter, 2 trevits, a copper boiler, a tea(sic) kettle, a stew pan and pair of bellows, two box irons and heaters, a scuttle, a three leg table, an oval table, a claw ditto, a joint stool, 8 ash chairs, 2 cupboards, 1 over the mantle, 2 flat irons, a brass mortar and pestle, a small sauce pan, 8 brass candlesticks, a pair of snuffers and stand, 6 iron candlesticks, a coffee pott and a chocolate pot, clock and case, a warming pan, a pair of stake tongs, a pair of tobacco tongs, 30 knives and forks, a glass mug and 8 tumblers, a coffee mill, a glass rummer, 7 gill 2 quart 3 pint 5 half pint decanters, 20 drinking glasses, a kettle and lamp, a tea chest, 3 punch ladles, a pewter measure

In the Bake House

An iron oven lid and peel, two oat bins, a shovel, 2 mathooks, beetle and wedges, a bill, a hammer and pinchers, some old lanthorns, a footman, 2 chairs, an axe and some other tools

In the Dish Room

Four pewter dishes, 14 plates, a form, a table, a plate rack, a cupboard, 3 wash tubs, dish tubs, a churn, a pail, 6 bowles, a tin dripping pan, 2 brass ladles, a skimmer, 3 saucepans, 3 pots and covers, a dish kettle, some tin and wood ware, a pair of slings and a man's saddle

In the Small beer Cellar

A stand, a bin, 2 tubs, a brass cock, a side saddle, a man's ditto, some earthenware and some old iron

In the Pantry

Three large powdering tubs, tin stands, a keeler, 7 stone jars, 10 crocks, some other pieces of earthenware, a frying pan, a dripping pan stand, 70 stone of pork, 40 pound of lard and some apples

In the Brewhouse and Yard

A large copper and iron work as fixed, 1 smaller ditto, a mash tub, a tun tub and 2 coolers as fixt, a large two-ear'd tub and an oval keeler, 2 hogsheads, 2 barrels, 1 kilderkin, a ferkin, a poker, a spade, 2 forms, 2 pails, 2 bowles, an iron kettle, a pigging, a hopbasket, a cock, a tun tub, 2 hogsheads, 2 smaller ditto, a funnell, 3 old stands, a hogtub, 3 old forms, 1 old pipe, 2 old tubs, a sieve, a bottle rack, a grindstone, a wheelbarrow, an iron back, a flasket and a stone bottle

In the Strong Beer Cellar

5 woodbound pipes, 11 hogsheads, a barrel, a kilderkin, 5 stands, 3 cocks, 6 stone bottles, 13 hogsheads, 4 small tubs, 3 stands, 2 cocks, a copper tunnel, 1,331 gallons of strong beer, 38 gallons of small beer, 5 gallons of brandy, 2 gallons of rum and 1 gallon of shrubb

China and Delf Ware

A large china bowl, one ditto, 3 smaller, ditto 7 basons, 12 cups, 8 saucers, 5 larger ditto, 10 plates, 1 crewit stand, several pieces of Delf Ware and some tin canisters

Linen

11 pair of sheets, 17 pillowbiers, 6 small table cloths, 1 large ditto, 10 napkins, 4 caps, 4 towels 14 pair of old sheets and 3 small table cloths

Plate

2 silver salts, a milk pot, 13 teaspoons, a pair of tea tongs and 2 tablespoons

Two Post Chaise and harness

37 bottles of wine

A RURAL IDYLL? – FROM THE MIDDLE AGES TO THE INDUSTRIAL REVOLUTION

Stock etc. on the Farm

6 horses, a cow, 2 fat hogs, 7 store pigs, 12 acres of wheat, 6 acres of young seeds, all the dressings and half dressings, all the fallows, some mould laid in Compass field, a stack of wheat, all the corn **in the barn**, a stump of hay, the oats in the granary, oats in the bin and beans in the bin, a malt mill, a pocket of hops, a half bushel, 3 gallon and 2 pottle measures, a screen, a parcell of chairs, harness **in the granary**

28 sacks, 1 dung mixon and dung in the yard, a parcell of wood and faggots, 2 carts, 3 harrows, a plow and tackle, 5 cart harness, 4 plow harness, a small cart, a ladder, a cyder mill and press, some sea coal, 5 stocks of bees, a chaff mound, 2 chaff sieves, 2 dozen of brooms, a wynch, 4 sewes a bushell measure, a shaul, a barn shovel, 6 prongs, 3 spuds, 1 mow cutter, 2 shovels, a spade, a matt hook, 4 old chaise weels, a parcel of lumber **in the Cart House**. A sythe and hook, a swap, a roller and a wheelbarrow

All the before-mentioned goods are valued at the sum of   £537.18s.7d

(Above) St John's Church *c.*1798 and (Right) before 1808. Notice the changes to the tower

Photographed in 1911 by Edgar Sharp in his collection of Surrey churches from watercolours by Henry Petrie 1790-1808

Another interesting document that has survived is the survey of the manor made by Isaac Messeder in 1762, who was commissioned to undertake it by Sir Edward de Bouverie's grandson, Viscount Folkestone. Two later maps, that of John Rocque (1764) and Thomas Bainbridge (1785) reveal the village as a collection of scattered small farms, with only the sub-manor of Hooley retaining any importance, and the village centred on Bradmore Green, now a conservation area. About a mile to the north of Hooley were the parish church of St John and the old court. The field names are enlightening. Some of them, like 'Old Peter's Three Score Acres' bear the name of earlier tenants. Others describe the terrain or the nature of the soil: The Goss (gorse), Starve Larke, Stoneyfield are examples. Some give a clue to land management – e.g Marl Field and Marling Pitt Hill. Others suggest

Extract from 'A Plan of an Estate within the Manor and Parish of Coulsdon in the County of Surrey together with the Boundary of the said Manor belonging to Thomas Byron Esqre. Made in 1785 by Tho. Bainbridge'

crafts such as 'Wimble Stimble' – a country name for the Crested Dog's Tail grass *Cynosurus cristatus* advocated by William Cobbett for the making of straw hats. There is an indication of enclosure in other field names, for example 'New Field'; and there are references to 'Common field pieces now enclosed', and 'A piece of Hooley Common now enclosed'. The main crops grown were oats, wheat, barley, peas and turnips.

In 1788 the population was estimated at about 300 and the acres under cultivation 3040.

On Coulsdon Common stood the village Ale House – *The Old Fox* – and two windmills. The house adjoining one of the mills still stands though the windmills have long since gone. The blacksmith's forge stood at the corner of Coulsdon Road and Waddington Avenue – the site is now occupied by a garage – and the wheelwright's cottage is still to be found at the northern end of the Common, near Stites Hill Road.

Smitham Bottom was by repute at this time a lonely, desolate area, the haunt of highwaymen and a camping place for gypsies – there are several references in the parish records to burials of 'travellers' and baptisms and often subsequent burials of their children. However, *The Red Lion* Inn was already indicated on maps of the area as early as 1735. Cricket matches were played on Lion Green and prize fights were held.

This then was the village, rural, quiet and somewhat isolated, with the main road through Smitham Bottom merely a lane, when the manor came into the hands of Thomas Byron – the first of the Byron dynasty to hold the Lordship of the Manor for the next 140 years – in 1782 .

The Old Fox Public House in 1890

The Parsonage in 1823 painted by John Hassell. Formerly the rectory of St John's, it was lived in by Revd Drummond at the time, although there is no evidence that he was the Reverend of Coulsdon Parish. The building was replaced by a stone building in 1841 and became a private residence, known as 'Parsons Pightle'. The building was destroyed in the 1960s

Courtesy of Croydon Art Collection
Croydon Clocktower

SOURCES

BANNERMAN, W B (Ed) (1910) *The Parish Registers of Coulsdon in the County of Surrey*

BRIGGS, A (1994) *A Social History of England* Weidenfeld & Nicolson

BROADBENT, U & LATHAM, R (Eds) (1976) *Coulsdon – a Downland Village*

MITCHELL, R (1981) *The Carews of Beddington* Sutton Libraries & Arts Services

SAALER, M (1989) *East Surrey Manors*. The Bourne Society

MALDEN, H E (Ed) (1902-1912) *Victoria County History of the County of Surrey*

WALFORD, E (1983) *Village London Part 3 – South East & South* Alderman Press

Chapter 6

Victorian Coulsdon

by Roger Packham

There is much information on the Victorian era in *Coulsdon – Downland Village* and in some of the other chapters in this book. It is also instructive to consult contemporary newspapers and what follows is largely based on that source.

DEVELOPMENT

Although the Victorian era witnessed few changes to the agricultural way of life of Coulsdon, notable developments were taking place in the Smitham Bottom valley where, traditionally, the only buildings were Hooley House, *The Red Lion* and Stoats Nest Farm. The London & Brighton railway line opened in 1841 but in 1839 the following had appeared—

> NEW TURNPIKE ROAD – The new line of turnpike road from Hooley House to near *The Star*, is expected to be opened in the course of a month; when finished it will complete the alteration of the road in that part of Hooley Lane. The alteration of the road near Merstham will, when finished, complete the deviations of turnpike roads in Surrey.

The new road and railway had little immediate impact; the 1851 Census recorded a Coulsdon population of 713 – this included parts of the parish which are now in Kenley and Purley. The old established farms of Tollers, Taunton, Bradmore, Portnalls, Placehouse, Stoats Nest, Woodplace, Hartley and Coulsdon Court were benevolently looked over by Thomas Byron and – from 1863 – Edmund Byron, together with the clergy from St John's. Marlpit Farm (now 22 Marlpit Lane) claims a date of 1878, and the new Cane Hill Asylum had its own farm from 1883.

The other buildings in the parish were scattered cottages, the forge and windmills, almshouses and workhouse; the inns, the church, the school and a handful of gentlemen's houses. They were surrounded by farmland and open spaces, but the rural serenity was about to be disturbed by the development of the Smitham Bottom valley. In April 1878 the purchase of Portnalls Farm was announced for the purpose of building the third Surrey lunatic asylum and the workforce involved in the construction can be imagined by the following notice from 1880—

Coulsdon Workhouse (near *The Fox* Public House) built in 1805, photographed in 2000

Marlpit Lane lin the Edwardian era

Marlpit Farm appears centre right

Coulsdon Almshouses, Coulsdon Road, built by Edmund Byron in the 1870s

Photographed 1929

Courtesy of Purley Library

Cane Hill Asylum built in 1883

Photographed in 2000

At the Croydon Petty Sessions, an application was made on behalf of Mr Brooks, landlord of *The Red Lion*, Smitham Bottom, for a kind of continuous licence for the sale of beer in a shanty at the new lunatic asylum works at Coulsdon. It may be remembered that a month or two back, Mr Brooks applied for an ordinary licence to the shanty, but it was refused on the ground that the magistrates had no power to grant the application. It was now stated that occasional licences were granted by the Epsom Bench for a similar building on Banstead Downs. Mr Brooks said that 200 to 300 men were at work on the new asylum and the men were actually leaving because of the absence of refreshment of the character it was now sought to supply. (Application refused).

The construction of Cane Hill led to more building work in Brighton Road, Chipstead Valley Road and Lion Green Road, which proved to be the end of the old Lion Green. This historic venue of cricket matches and prize fights disappeared before the developer, and the pond was filled in. It is regrettable that there does not appear to be a pictorial record of Lion Green.

Coulsdon and Cane Hill – now Coulsdon South – Station, built 1889, photographed looking south 1910

The present Coulsdon South station appeared in 1889; its location was influenced by the asylum and the new houses in the Reddown Road area. Seven years before the station was opened the following notice appeared (1882)—

50 PLOTS and valuable FREEHOLD BUILDING LAND, forming part of the HOOLEY HOUSE ESTATE, possessing very important frontages on the main Brighton Road, close to a contemplated new station, and where, from local improvements, a great demand for residence and cottage property is apparent.

Ashdown Park Hotel, formerly Hooley House, demolished in 1971

In the same year, the Postmaster General, Henry Fawcett, sanctioned arrangements under which a post office would be established in Smitham Bottom and, at an Extraordinary General Meeting of the Caterham Spring Water Company 'there was great promise of an extension of business in the Caterham and Kenley Valley, about the region called Stoats Nest.'

In 1883, Cane Hill was established and the contractor was anxious to leave the site. The following auction notice gives some idea of the extent of the building operation—

To Contractors, builders etc.

SMITHAM BOTTOM, COULSDON – Mr J T Chappell's Offices, Sheds and Stables, Cane Hill Asylum near *The Red Lion Hotel*

auction of

Brick and Tile erections comprising general offices, the canteen, the stables, the clerk of the works office.

Weather board and felt roof constructions: engine shed with brick pit; Mill and Carpenter's shop; Lime Shed; Mortar Shed; 3 Smiths Shops; Portable Office, two useful horses, iron cisterns, trollies, sleepers, new and old doors and sashes.

500 Scaffold poles, 300 scaffold boards, 5 dobbins, barrows, putlogs, trestles, a large quantity of centres, 20 stacks of good firewood and various miscellaneous effects.

In November 1883 tenders were invited for the supply of milk to the 'New Surrey Lunatic Asylum which is constructed to receive over 1100 patients. The milk will have to be delivered in such quantities as may be required at Caterham Junction (Purley) Railway Station twice daily.'

Further development was likely in 1883, for in that year a Bill for a proposed new railway from the Brighton line to Upper Caterham passed its second reading in the House of Lords. The stumbling block, though, was Edmund Byron and his beloved foxes, and although the scheme was subsequently revived the non-appearance of the railway preserved the rural aspect of the parish away from Brighton Road until after the Squire's death in 1921. The railway line to Kingswood was opened in 1897, and Smitham Station was opened on this line in 1904. Smitham thus became the third local railway station, appearing five years after the new Stoats Nest (later Coulsdon North) Station.

At the turn of the century, Smitham Bottom (the Coulsdon of today) had assumed its present character, minus the traffic problems. Housing in the proximity of *The Red Lion* was modest and more cottage style housing appeared in the early 1900s along Chipstead Valley Road. There were larger houses close to Coulsdon South Station but the grandest houses arrived on Smitham Downs where large Edwardian houses were built from The Avenue to Smitham Downs Road and along Brighton Road.

AGRICULTURE AND INDUSTRY

The agricultural nature of the parish is apparent from sales notices in newspapers. Thus in 1839 Mr Bleaden of Coulsdon Court Farm was selling corn, hay, straw, live and dead stock from his farm and those of Stoats Nest and Hartley. In 1843, Woodplace Farm with farmhouse, 224 acres and right of pasturage on an adjoining down were to be let and three years later the following appeared—

COULSDON, SURREY

To Timber Merchants, Builders, Bricklayers & Others

MESSRS NASH

ARE instructed to sell by auction at *The Red Lion* at Smitham Bottom on 10 June, 390 ASH ENDS, 134 ELM do, a few ASH, BEECH and OAK ENDS and 80,000 BUILDING BRICKS, divided into Lots for the convenience of purchasers, as the same are now lying upon Waterhouse, Tollworth *(sic)*, Hartley and Portnalls Farms at Coulsdon.

The bricks are at the Brick Field, near Coulsdon Church.

Mr John Gilbert, the bailiff upon the estate at Portnalls Farm, will show the timber...

**Mr John Gilbert,
Bailiff**

*Photograph courtesy of
Mrs Lucy Butler*

If the brickfield represents a transition from agriculture to industry, this trend was expanded in 1865 when Hall & Co erected a brick-built gas-fired kiln as an experiment which heralded the presence of the lime works.

In 1846, the following notice indicates some house building activity, perhaps as a result of the sale of bricks—

COTTAGES FOR AGRICULTURAL LABOURERS – We have lately noticed some neat and most convenient dwellings erected at Coulsdon, by Thomas Keen Esq of Croydon, for his labourers. Each cottage consists of a room nearly six yards square, a nice pantry, a kitchen with oven and copper, a wood room with other conveniences, and a nice piece of garden ground. There are two doors behind and two bedrooms. The rent is only 2s.0d a week. We need scarcely observe the inmates looked clean, comfortable and contented. Mr Keen did not build as an investment, but that his men and families should be comfortably housed.

Agriculture was not confined to the farms, and in 1864 James Banks of *The Fox* had 'constantly on sale dry stacked hurdles, wattles, sheep cages, stakes and bavins of all sorts.' The gentlemen's houses were also engaged in agriculture and even horticulture: in 1882 there was a sale at Hooley House of glasshouses and choice standard orange trees, whilst the following from 1876 gives an idea of life at The Grange—

THE GRANGE, COULSDON... The lease of this good Residence and 14 acres to be disposed of: three large reception rooms, ten bedrooms, two dressing rooms, day and night nurseries, good offices, stabling for four horses and farm buildings. Rent £130 per annum. Premium £150. Apply to Mr Richard Martin, Surveyor, Caterham.

The windmill on the Common – a painting by Thomas Whittle

Built in 1777, it ceased working in 1893 and was demolished in 1924

Courtesy of Croydon Art Collection, Croydon Clocktower

Cottages at Tollers Farm, which were demolished in 1935

Photograph c. 1934
Courtesy of Purley Library

Farthing Downs, Coulsdon

View from Farthing Downs
***c.*1905**
The houses on the left are in Fairdene Road

It was, however, the farms that continued the long-established agricultural practices. In 1868 Portnalls Farm advertised its annual sale of fat sheep and in 1880,

TOLLERS FARM, COULSDON

C & F Rutley will sell by auction, by direction of Mr A Strachan, who is quitting,

The Valuable Live and Dead Farming Stock, comprising 9 cart horses, grey cart mare and foal, well-bred 3 year old nag filly, 5 cows, 4 fat calves, the flock of Hampshire Down Ewes and Lambs, comprising 160 ewes, 120 lambs, 2 rams and 2 ram lambs; 6 young turkeys and numerous useful implements and effects; also 30 quarters of black oats.

The Coulsdon windmills on Stites Hill Road were of great importance to an agricultural parish. The earlier mill was sited where Windmill House now stands, and 100 yards distant – opposite Windmill Cottage – stood the second mill, which survived until 1924. Alexander Tutt, one of the last millers, was told on arrival in 1872 that the latter mill had arrived a century previously, but its origin was unknown. The Russell family held the mills from 1826-1861 but for eight years from 1845 the windmills and the 122 acre Taunton Farm and outbuildings were leased to James Dives, formerly of Merstham. He is shown in the 1851 Census as a 58 year-old master miller employing two men, including Jacob Webb, a loader and miller who lodged at the premises. An auction notice from 1849 describes Taunton Farm and windmills—

FREEHOLD ESTATE, of about 121 Acres, including two capital Post Windmills and suitable Dwellings and buildings. A COMPACT FREEHOLD PROPERTY, called Taunton's Farm, situate near Coulsdon Church, in which there is a family pew, comprising a good homestead and buildings, with nearly 115 acres of arable, meadow and woodland in the occupation of Mr George Hoare, under lease at £100 p.a., also the two windmills, known as Coulsdon Mills.

ACCIDENTS

A glimpse of life in Victorian Coulsdon can be gleaned from newspapers, sometimes when unfortunate accidents occurred. There were two such events in 1839—

An accident occurred on the Brighton Railway on Monday, to a lad about 16 years of age, who was run over, while drawing one of the chalk carts from the cutting at the back of *The Red Lion*, Smitham Bottom, to the filling-up of the hollow, near Coulsdon Lane, by which one of his legs was broken in two places. The fractures were so severe that amputation was necessary.

The second accident that year was recorded as follows—

SMITHERS BOTTOM COACH ACCIDENT

Friday, 23 August, between 4 and 5, as *The Wonder*, Brighton coach, was on its way to town, near *The Red Lion* Inn at this place, one of the fore wheels came off and the coach immediately turned over. It was heavily laden with passengers and luggage and the whole of the former were thrown to the ground with great violence, but, providentially, none of them received any further injury than being severely bruised and of course very much alarmed at the accident. The coachman sprang from the box and seized the horses' heads, and with the assistance of some of the Brighton Railroad policemen, who were on the spot, succeeded in effectually restraining them from dashing away with the coach, which in the first instance they had attempted to do. It was found upon examination that the underpart of the vehicle was so much injured that it could not proceed on its journey, and an express was despatched to Croydon for another coach, which was speedily obtained, and the passengers and luggage of *The Wonder* were conveyed by it to town. The arrival of the passengers in London was delayed by the accident for upwards of two hours.

Another accident on the railway at Stoats Nest was reported in 1847 and in 1862 two gangers were buried alive by an earth fall during excavations near Stoats Nest Station. The inquest was held at *The Red Lion*.

In 1890 a horse-drawn vehicle ran into the Forge Pond, Lacey Green and a woman passenger was drowned. If water could prove hazardous, fire was an ever-present danger. The following comes from 1870, when Stoats Nest Farm was struck by lightning—

ALARMING FIRE AT STOATS NEST

The storm which after so long a period of drought passed over the neighbourhood of Croydon on Thursday evening left a lurid mark of its course by the lightning setting fire to a stack yard. Shortly after ten o'clock, when the air was oppressive in the extreme, and vivid flashes of lightning, accompanied by the distant sound of thunder, was seemingly illuminating the heavens every minute, the southern part was illumined by the red glare of a large fire, in the direction of what was once familiarly known as Beggar's Bush. The volunteer firemen at The Broadway engine-station were not slow in discovering the fact, and, as from their observatory at the top of the house, it could be seen that the fire was at a distance they at once started with their engine and hose-truck to the scene of the conflagration without waiting for the usual 'call'.

They found the fire to be at the farm in the occupation of Mr Gideon Smith; that the fire had spread from the stack which had been struck by the lightning to the entire homestead. Fire engines were not of much use in such a place as Stoats Nest Farm; there are no ponds and the only water available was from a pump on the premises, scarce sufficient to provide for domestic wants. The Croydon volunteers, however, at once set to work, and pumping into a trough kept their engine going as fast as they could. By keeping the house cool they succeeded in saving it from the flames, but the destruction of property was otherwise very deplorable.

The fire raged from about ten o'clock till one, when that portion of the outbuildings not quite consumed by the fire, was saved by the bursting of the storm overhead, and the descent of torrents of rain. Such was the reflection of the fire at a distance, that shortly after the Croydon engine had started, the engines from South Norwood and Crystal Palace rattled through the town on their way to the scene: while the Carshalton volunteers were out with their engine from across country, soon followed by the Tooting engine. With the exception, however, of the Croydon engine, the firemen had to return without working, from the aforesaid want of water. The premises and contents were insured in the Imperial and County Fire offices and when at about half past three o'clock, the firemen returned, it was found that two cottages, three barns, three outbuildings, three straw stacks and one hay stack had been consumed.

Other reported accidents range from Squire Byron falling from his horse in 1896 and 1898, to the tragic death of J C Pickersgill-Cunliffe of Hooley House at Caterham Junction Station (Purley) in 1873, in the days before the subway was built. In the Edwardian era, Stoats Nest Station (Coulsdon North) also witnessed tragedy and this is discussed in the chapter on Transport.

CRIME

It is easy to imagine that Coulsdon, under the benevolent if autocratic rule of the Byrons, was an ideal parish with contented farmers and workers. It was not always so.

Not surprisingly there are several reports of criminal deeds at *The Red Lion*. In 1840 Charlotte Towers was charged with robbing the landlord, Henry Nokes, whilst in 1870 when George Milne, the licensee, was convicted of assaulting and beating George Crosier, a carpenter of Caterham Junction (Purley), after they had been drinking at the Caterham Junction Hotel (later *The Railway Hotel*). Milne made some allusion to having paid some scamp of a carpenter 8d an hour and struck Crosier in the eye with his fist and on the mouth and head with the butt end of his whip. Despite the conviction for assault Milne retained his licence the following year.

In 1882 Arthur Rathbone of South Croydon was summoned by Thomas Brooks, landlord of *The Red Lion*, for being drunk and refusing to leave. He was found guilty of indecent conduct and obscene language and 'a more disgusting case never came before the Croydon bench.'

In 1874 George Browning, labourer of Coulsdon, was summoned for assault by John Roach, station master at Caterham Junction (Purley) when a witness was Sam Sturgess, booking clerk. Francis Coomber, a labourer of Smitham Bottom, twice appeared before the Croydon bench in 1883 for being drunk, disorderly and assaulting a policeman. Another labourer that year, Harry Gye from Smitham Bottom, was charged with stealing a half sovereign from a trunk at Elizabeth Cottages, Smitham Bottom. At the same cottages in the following year, Catherine, wife of John Norris, an engineer at Cane Hill Asylum, committed suicide, and the inquest was held at *The Red Lion*. Twenty years earlier, in 1864, the locality had been shocked at another suicide when the body of an 18 year-old under-housemaid at Mr Pickersgill's Hooley House was found down a well. The inquest was again held at *The Red Lion*.

It is not surprising that there were cases of petty theft, and in 1844 Mary Ann Gatland, Charlotte Etherington and Mary Lover appeared in court to answer the complaint of farmer James Brown for stealing bushes. The outcome of the case is not recorded but the three ladies together with farmer Brown all appear in the 1851 census.

A case of lamb-stealing was reported in 1864 and in 1882 Martha Ridgers, a garden woman, was charged with stealing 2s.6d from a barn at Coulsdon, the property of Louisa Divine. Ms Divine had slept in the barn on Mr Lingard's farm with eight or nine men described as farmworkers and tramps and the case was brought to the attention of the sanitary inspector. Five years earlier, Joseph Linger, farmer of Coulsdon and possibly the owner of the insanitary barn, charged Joseph Tucker, stockbroker of Portnalls, with cruelty to a sheep but the case was dismissed. In 1883 Richard Underwood, blacksmith of Park Terrace, Sanderstead, was charged with stealing two dead rabbits from Portnalls Farm, the property of Joseph Tucker.

Occasionally violence was evident; a knifing case at Portnalls Farm came to court in 1873 and in 1882 Joseph Bullen of Westow Hill, was charged with violently assaulting William Skelton near Farthing Downs, where five men had been ferreting.

Sentences were invariably harsh and when James Alexander Douglas was burgled at Coulsdon Grange in 1873 the offender was ordered to do 14 years' penal servitude.

The great era of agricultural unrest was in the 1830s, though not notably at Coulsdon, and it is something of a surprise to come across the following from *The Croydon Advertiser* in 1883. The report presumably refers to Tollers Farm and Edmund Byron was doubtless the owner and not the occupier—

COULSDON   INCENDIARISM

At two minutes to three o'clock on Saturday morning last, the Croydon Corporation Fire Brigade were summoned to a fire at Tollard's *(sic)* Farm, Coulsdon in the occupation of Mr Edmund Byron JP, Lord of the Manor. The steamer was at once despatched to the farm, which is situate about six miles from Croydon. The fire had been raging since the previous evening, the bailiff explaining that he did not send for the engines because there was not a drop of water in the neighbourhood. Superintendent Tennuci found this to be the case. Other engines afterwards arrived from Croydon and Norwood, but of course their services were not available, and all the firemen could do was to save what property they could by removal. The amount of damage is as follows: Two stacks of straw of about 30 loads totally destroyed; brick and timber built barn, 120ft by 36ft and contents consisting of hay, straw and about 30 sacks of oats; brick and stone built building, used as cart shed and stabling, and contents all burned out and fallen down; and open cow-shed and stables adjoining damaged by fire, and roof by breakage. Estimated damage about £1,500. Contents insured in the Sun Fire Office for £1,100. The cause of the fire is supposed to be incendiarism.

None of the above cases can be described as other than petty crime, and historically the most important legal case of the period concerns the worthy squire and his unsuccessful attempts to enclose the commons. The decisive victory of William Hall over Edmund Byron deserves the unfailing gratitude of all.

SOCIAL AND LEISURE

Edmund Byron's passion for hunting involved many of the estate workers, and details may be seen from his hunting journals, farming accounts and game books. His reign as master of the Old Surrey Hounds commenced in 1876 but was not always without incident; in 1896 he was carried home on a brougham after a fall at Farleigh which resulted in a cut on his head, and he suffered another fall less than 18 months later.

COULSDON
Industrial Exhibition.

AN EXHIBITION OF
SPECIMENS OF HANDIWORK

SUCH AS

DRAWING, PAINTING, NEEDLEWORK, WOOD CARVING, MODELLING, CARPENTRY, &c.,

AND OTHER ARTICLES.

BY PARISHIONERS OF COULSDON,

WILL BE HELD AT

THE SCHOOL, BRADMORE GREEN,

ON

APRIL 10TH AND 11TH, 1890,

OPEN from 2 p.m. to 9 p.m.

ADMISSION 6d. each till 6 o'clock; after 6, 3d.

Tea with Bread & Butter & Cake will be provided at 6d. a head till 7 p.m.

Advertisement for an exhibition held on Bradmore Green in April 1890 and arranged by Mrs Byron

VICTORIAN COULSDON

The East Surrey Agricultural Association's annual ploughing match and meeting for rewarding labourers and servants was occasionally held locally, and in 1840 it was staged at Coulsdon Court on a piece of land called Chankey Gravel, belonging to Charles Bleaden. In 1870 when the same event was held at Addington Lodge Farm, the winners of prizes for ploughing included Coulsdon men Frederick Nash and Richard Bashford in Mr Byron's employ, and William Church and Daniel Doulton in S N Rowland's employ. Prizes for labourers in husbandry who had brought up the largest family without parochial aid were won by Russell Martingale (sen) and George Jeffery, both employed by James Brown, and Joseph Whiteborn who was employed by Mr Rowland.

In 1844 there is a report of the Surrey Harriers chasing a hare across Farthing Downs and beyond, whilst in 1870 the Surrey Staghounds' chase of a stag 'carted near the kennel at Smitham Bottom' appears, but the hounds were transferred to Chilmead Farm in 1879.

Musical references are scarce, but the Coulsdon United Services Band is reported as playing at a dinner at *The Blacksmith's Arms*, Caterham in 1871. Further leisure activities were doubtless arranged at public houses and in 1850 a meeting of the British United Friendly Society took place at *The Fox*, courtesy of landlord James Banks.

Athletic sports were secondary to hunting pursuits, but there are regular reports of cricket matches against other villages throughout the Victorian period: in 1859 and 1861 cricket was played at the harvest home at Coulsdon Court by Thomas Byron's employees. A running ground was opened in 1882 opposite *The Red Lion,* and bowls was being played near that public house in 1913.

The study of archaeology can be described as a leisure activity of the Victorian gentleman and in 1871 J Wickham Flower with Granville Leveson-Gower opened barrows on Farthing Downs.

Church matters commanded the attention of local gentlemen, and the rise of the new churches is detailed elsewhere. At St John's, in 1871, the parish churchyard was extended in a ceremony presided over by the Bishop of Winchester who on the same day presided over the opening of All Saints' Church, Kenley. An even more important day occurred in 1883 when the Lord Mayor of London, with a guard of honour, dedicated the local commons as open spaces in perpetuity.

Bishop of Southwark dedicating St Andrew's Church site 1913

The following report conveys something of a day's leisure in Victorian Coulsdon (1859)—

A DAY AT THE SQUIRE'S

We had a very pleasant day at Mr Byron's on Tuesday last. There was a good game of cricket with men and boys in two different places. The beautiful park and gardens were thrown open to all and the number of visitors was very great. About 150 sat down to a first-rate dinner, of which roast and boiled beef and plum pudding formed the staple. After the cloth was removed the usual loyal toasts were given. Mr Banks then proposed the healths of Thomas Byron Esq, Mrs Byron and family. He rose, he said, to propose a toast which he was sure they would join heartily in responding to... They were all invited there today for amusement, and also to partake of good old English fare – roast beef and plum pudding... He could not refrain from noticing the kind and liberal way in which this treat was given, because it showed that it flowed from a good heart and good feeling towards the workmen and their wives, the tenants and their wives, and the servants too *(loud cheers)*. He hoped and trusted that the founder of this feast might be spared, with Mrs Byron and family, for many years to come... There was plenty of right good malt and hops on the board, and, after dinner, music and dancing were kept up with spirit until the rain came on. The party then retired into a booth, erected for the purpose, capable of holding 200 persons. Thos Byron Esq, the Revd C Randolph, Mr Tanner and many other friends of Mr Byron's waited on the party until dinner was over. The booth was neatly decorated; 'God Save the Queen' was formed in large letters at the top, and 'Peace and plenty' at the bottom, with a profusion of flowers. The health of Mr Gilbert was drunk by his friends in the best spirit. The rain kept the party rather late for shelter, but all passed off without an oath or a murmur from anyone, each hoping to meet again on the same occasion.

SOURCES

BROADBENT, U & LATHAM, R (Eds) (1976) *Coulsdon – Downland Village.* Bourne Society

Caterham & Purley Weekly Press 1913

Croydon Advertiser 1870-83

DOBSON, C G (1951) *A Century and a Quarter*. Hall & Co Ltd

FARRIES, K G & MASON, M T *The Windmills of Surrey & Inner London.* C Skilton

Sussex Agricultural Express 1839-68

Westerham Herald 1896-98

———————————————————————

Chapter 7

The Byrons of Coulsdon

by Ian Scales

The Byrons are the most significant family in Coulsdon. Over two centuries, their names recur throughout this book as the major landowners and driving force of Coulsdon Manor. They were the only squires to live in this manor while they owned it, and in their time they shaped the lives of their tenants and gave us – albeit at times unwillingly – the superb open spaces we enjoy today. But who were they?

Of a family that can trace its roots back to the time of William the Conqueror, the Coulsdon Byrons are of the same stock as the famous 6th Baron (Lord) Byron, the romantic poet of Napoleonic times; witness their heraldic arms, described below. The Coulsdon Byrons married into the Jeffreys family in both the 18th and 19th centuries and that family, amongst other historical personages, can boast the infamous Judge Jeffreys responsible for the 'Bloody Assizes' that marked the end of the unsuccessful Monmouth rebellion in 1685.

Lord Byron's descendants bear an Achievement of Arms, the shield of which is blazoned as 'Argent three bendlets enhanced gules' which, in English, means a background to the shield of silver (argent) with three narrow red (gules) stripes running from top left to middle right (bendlets), being lifted above the middle of the shield (enhanced). The Coulsdon branch has inherited a similar shield differenced only by having an ermine background instead of silver. Both families use a mermaid as a crest on the helmet, differenced by Lord Byron's having one tail and the Coulsdon Byrons having two; also, Lord Byron's mermaid carries a comb and a mirror, whilst the Coulsdon family features an escutcheon of the arms in the right hand instead of the comb.

Both families use the same motto – not strictly part of the Achievement – which is the Latin 'Crede Byron', meaning 'Trust Byron'.

Arms granted 28 April 1787 to Thomas Byron

Thomas I (1738-1821) married well, and using his wife's money bought the 385 acres of Coulsdon Manor from the Earl of Radnor – grandson of Viscount Folkestone – in 1782 for £14,000. He had a number of houses, mostly in London, but seems to have lived and certainly died in Hooley House, having bought that sub-manor at the same time as Coulsdon. Every Sunday morning the family drove up Marlpit Lane to church at St John's, a man going before them to brush aside any twigs that might scratch the coach.

As with many of his rank and times, Thomas was a colonel in the Army, in his case the Grenadiers, 3rd Regiment of Foot Guards. In 1777 the Regiment was due to be posted to fight in the American War of Independence, which prompted his wife to write—

Lucy Ann Byron, based on a contemporary portrait

'Monday late at night: Dear Mr Byron,

I beg for God's sake you will remember you *promised* to make me happy. I must be miserable if you go to America, if you are well & safe at home I shall be happy .... Don't ask advice, if my happiness is your meaning.

Yours affectionately, L A Byron.'

No immediate reply was forthcoming, prompting more letters asking him to 'Pray send me a kind answer'. In response to his wife's plea Colonel Thomas quit the Army on 16 January 1778 instead of going out to fight in the Colonies.

He married Lucy (*née* Whetham) in 1770 but they had no children and following her death in 1796 he married again, to Miss Harriet Latham. When he died in 1821 his estate passed to his younger brother **Col. Richard Byron** of the Coldstream Guards with the understanding that it be passed on to Richard's son.

Thomas II (1772-1845) son of Col. Richard married Louisa Brassey, the heiress daughter of a London banker and became the MP for Hertford. His sister Charlotte married the Revd John Jeffreys. When Thomas died his son **Thomas III** (1809-1863) succeeded as squire and it was he who built Coulsdon Court on Hartley Farm in the 1850s, in the process cutting off the Queen's Highway and demolishing Hartley Farm – such was the power he assumed as landowner. Thomas married his first cousin Julia Jeffreys (daughter of Charlotte and John) and their son **Edmund** (1843-1921) – who also married a first cousin, Charlotte Jeffreys, grand-daughter of Charlotte and John – inherited the estate in 1862 at the age of 19. It was by then some 2000 acres.

Thomas Byron II, aged 34, and Louisa Brassey, aged 28

From portraits painted in 1806 to celebrate their marriage

Nobby, as Edmund was known, laid the foundation stone of Coulsdon Court in 1850 when he was six years old on the instructions of his father Thomas, and in his turn reigned – no other word will do – from the Court as squire until 1921. In those 58 years as Lord of the Manor he had virtually no one to say him nay, which had a definite effect on a naturally autocratic character. He met Kaiser Wilhelm II of Germany while on a fishing trip in Norway, resulting in his being invited to hunt with the Royal party in the Grünewald forest near Berlin.

None of his six children, in his opinion, chose the right partner in marriage and his (and his wife's) refusals to meet new family members were a continuing irritant. Lucy, their eldest child, was born eight months after their marriage and was presumably premature! When she was old enough, her parents took a house in London for the Season where she met and fell in love with Theodore Hall Hall, thus fulfilling the point of Lucy's 'coming out'.

(Above left) Julia Byron (née Jeffreys), Edmund's mother; *(Above right)* Edmund as a young man;
(Below left) Charlotte Emily Byron (née Jeffreys), Edmund's wife; *(Below right)* Edmund in later life

COULSDON COURT GOLF CLUB HOUSE. 20

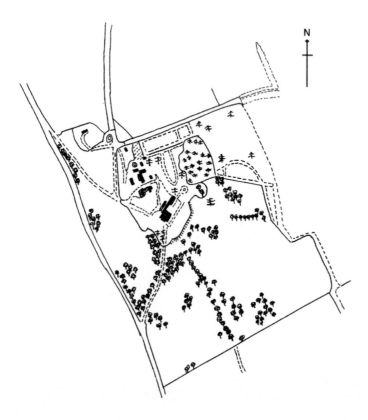

N

(Above) **The Court House that Thomas Byron built in 1850, later Coulsdon Court Golf Club House and now Coulsdon Manor Hotel**

(Left) **Plan of Coulsdon Court Estate, based on the 1868 Ordnance Survey map**

THE BYRONS OF COULSDON

Despite his being a barrister with an Eton and Oxford background and a member of the Athenaeum to boot, Theodore was not considered suitable by the Byrons, and it took a long time of persistent wooing of the family before he was allowed to wed his sweetheart.

A Victorian in many ways, Edmund had a cold bath every morning of his life. He held daily morning prayers for family and staff. Card games, even patience, were forbidden on Sundays, when he attended church twice during the day. A grass path was carefully kept by the ploughmen between house and church so that he could walk to services. He gave land for an extension to the graveyard and paid for a new organ. He built and maintained the almshouses in the village and gave each occupant 2s.6d a week in addition to what they received under the poor law. In harsh seasons his tenant farmers received a remission of rent. His father having granted the land for a new school (now Bradmore Green Primary) in 1845, Edmund kept the school in funds for many years.

However, he could be possessive about his land. He wished to enclose Farthing Downs in the 1870s and was opposed by William and James Hall in a notorious court case. It was not until the City of London Corporation stepped in and purchased the land from him that its future as common ground was ensured. Right to the end of his life he refused to give up land even for a memorial park. Eventually he did sell 11 acres in Marlpit Lane in 1920 for a fair sum, but considered £100 of the price to be his contribution to the park. When the Government wanted to build local 'homes fit for heroes' after World War I – now Stoats Nest Village – it had to obtain a compulsory purchase order before he would sell the land. He then set up a line of yew trees along Coulsdon Road to hide the view of houses containing tenants who were not of his choice.

Edmund lived for sport, not just the occasional trip to Germany with the Kaiser, but in June every year he would be off to Norway for the salmon season. He would take some of his staff and a set of silver and stay until the beginning of August. There were usually some young women in the party, though his wife stayed at home. He would be back for the opening of the partridge season on 1 September, then pheasants in October and hunting from 1 November, which lasted until the spring. This was followed by point-to-points until early summer, when he would usually go abroad to somewhere like Italy or Egypt. One year he went hunting in America, which trip accounted for two of the largest mounted heads on the walls of Coulsdon Court, a wapiti and a buffalo. Of all his sports, he loved hunting the best. He was Master of the Foxhounds of the Old Surrey for 25 years until 1903. In 1894 he had a bad fall at a point-to-point at Lingfield and had to give up the horn.

Edmund would have been very rich if he had not lost a great deal of money in a business before companies were limited by law. As it was he left £168,000 in spite of having had to live on his capital during his last years. Unfortunately he died in 1921 when there was a major slump in values, so the potentially very valuable property was sold for comparatively little.

When he died his coffin was borne by his tenant farmers from the house, across the 600 yards to St John's church while the tenor bell tolled 77 times, once for each of his years.

Squire Nobby's son **Cecil** predeceased his father in 1910. Cecil lived for years in Tenerife in an attempt to assuage the TB he suffered from for all of his adult life. As usual his choice of partner was objected to by his parents and he moved to Canada to avoid their baleful attitude, joining his elder brother Tom and hoping the dry climate of the prairies would suit him. His fiancée joined him there; they were married and lived on a farm he had bought near Calgary. A girl was born to them but only lived for three days. On hearing the news his mother wrote a heartless letter to him, saying—

> 'I fear you will have been sorry to lose your infant – perhaps had it lived you would have understood the feelings of a parent – I can only feel that it might have treated you someday as you have treated us, therefore happier for you that Providence took it in its infancy.'

with more in the same vein, only to be signed 'Your affectionate Mother'! Cecil led a blissful married life but died aged 39.

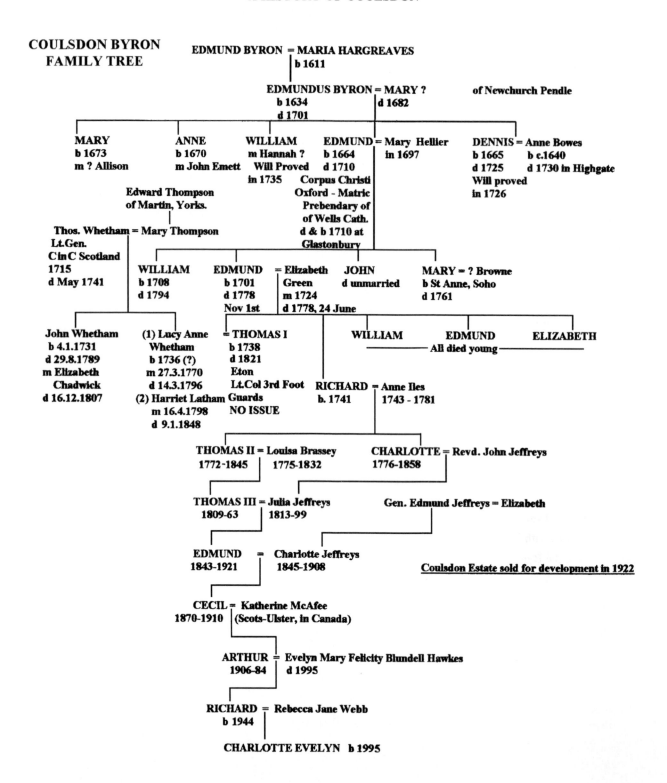

COULSDON BYRON FAMILY TREE

EDMUND BYRON = MARIA HARGREAVES
b 1611

EDMUNDUS BYRON = MARY ?
b 1634   d 1682   of Newchurch Pendle
d 1701

MARY	ANNE	WILLIAM	EDMUND = Mary Hellier	DENNIS = Anne Bowes
b 1673	b 1670	m Hannah ?	b 1664 in 1697	b 1665 b c.1640
m ? Allison	m John Emett	Will Proved	d 1710	d 1725 d 1730 in Highgate
		in 1735	Corpus Christi	Will proved
			Oxford - Matric	in 1726
			Prebendary of	
			of Wells Cath.	
			d & b 1710 at	
			Glastonbury	

Edward Thompson
of Martin, Yorks.

Thos. Whetham = Mary Thompson
Lt.Gen.
C in C Scotland
1715
d May 1741

WILLIAM   EDMUND   = Elizabeth   JOHN   MARY = ? Browne
b 1708   b 1701   Green   d unmarried   b St Anne, Soho
d 1794   d 1778   m 1724   d 1761
             Nov 1st   d 1778, 24 June

John Whetham   (1) Lucy Anne   = THOMAS I   WILLIAM   EDMUND   ELIZABETH
b 4.1.1731   Whetham   b 1738   ———— All died young ————
d 29.8.1789   b 1736 (?)   d 1821
m Elizabeth   m 27.3.1770   Eton
   Chadwick   d 14.3.1796   Lt.Col 3rd Foot
d 16.12.1807   (2) Harriet Latham Guards   RICHARD = Anne Iles
                   m 16.4.1798   NO ISSUE   b. 1741   1743 - 1781
                   d 9.1.1848

THOMAS II = Louisa Brassey   CHARLOTTE = Revd. John Jeffreys
1772-1845   1775-1832   1776-1858

THOMAS III = Julia Jeffreys   Gen. Edmund Jeffreys = Elizabeth
1809-63   1813-99

EDMUND   =   Charlotte Jeffreys   **Coulsdon Estate sold for development in 1922**
1843-1921   1845-1908

CECIL = Katherine McAfee
1870-1910 (Scots-Ulster, in Canada)

ARTHUR = Evelyn Mary Felicity Blundell Hawkes
1906-84   d 1995

RICHARD = Rebecca Jane Webb
b 1944

CHARLOTTE EVELYN   b 1995

Cecil also had a son **Arthur** who lived a full and Byronic life, resulting in his being described on his tombstone at St John's as 'Athlete, bonviveur and cognoscente'. He died in 1984 and is buried in St John's churchyard. Evelyn Mary Felicity Blundell Hawkes, Arthur's second wife, was born in Aldourie, a Scottish castle of the Frazer Tytler family. Her mother, a convert to Roman Catholicism, hated the fact that her daughter had married a divorced man and never really reconciled herself to the marriage. Arthur did not improve matters by inviting her to 'come and have a look at the little bastard', Richard, whom she absolutely adored. At first they lived in Cheshire and then shortly after World War II went to New Zealand before returning to Albert Hall Mansions, Sloane Street. She died aged 85 and was buried at St John's on 30 November 1995. During her life she was known as a film actress and also as a painter in oils, having exhibited several times at the Royal Academy.

Arthur's and Evelyn's son **Richard Evelyn**, born in 1944, lives in Oxfordshire and has a daughter, **Charlotte Evelyn**, the last of this line to date. Richard brought Charlotte to Coulsdon (he says the family always pronounced it 'Colesdon') in 1999 to show her the old family estates. The Byron squires, as abstracted from documents were—

Thomas Byron I	born 1738	bought Coulsdon Manor 1782	died 1821	No issue
Thomas Byron II	born 1772	son of Col. Richard Byron, (younger brother of Thomas I)		
		MP for Hertford	died 1845	
Thomas Byron III	born 1809	built Coulsdon Court	died 7.4.1863	aged 54
Edmund Byron	born 1843	Squire for 58 years The land was sold for development in 1922 under instructions in Edmund's will.	died 30.4.1921	aged 77

SOURCES

BYRON, A (1982) *A Short History of the Jeffreys and Byron Families*. Privately printed

Conversations with Richard Byron. 1999

Archives of the Byron Family held by Mrs L R Rohan Butler, Edmund's grand-daughter, as abstracted by Roger Packham and Ted Purver. 1990 (Typescript)

Chapter 8

World War I

by Roger Packham

A trawl through the columns of *The Coulsdon & Purley Weekly Record* provides a picture of how Coulsdon folk reacted to the harsh realities of the war.

It has been stated that Coulsdon's share in the Great War is part of the national story, not local history – a view not universally held. Early in the war, in August 1914, some local residents were accused of being selfish—

> 'The scenes that I have witnessed almost beggars description for the residents of Coulsdon are indeed passing through great troubles... but we must all bear the burden bravely and endeavour to assist each other in every way. I am afraid, however, in many instances the spirit of selfishness is being shown, especially by those people who have means and are using them to the disadvantage of their poorer neighbours by making large purchases of provisions, thus forcing up prices.'

In the same month it was reported that nearly 100 men from Coulsdon had been called to the colours, including 27 from Cane Hill and a large number from Netherne. The men left the neighbourhood amid hearty cheers from their friends, some of the parting from wives and children being 'very affecting.'

Anti-German feelings ran high and when Jacques Koshmann, an elderly German subject, failed to return a 'goodnight' from Henry Blandford in The Drive, he was taken to Kenley Police Station, but discharged. In the same month, an artist was arrested for sketching near the Asylum gates.

Still in August 1914 it was reported that an aeroplane passed over Coulsdon at a great height, travelling in the direction of Hendon, and in October much excitement was caused at Coulsdon by the appearance of several aeroplanes at Woodcote, where they were visited by many of the residents.

By this time Coulsdon had a national hero—

> 'THE NAVAL VICTORY – Commodore Goodenough, who is in command of the Light Cruiser Squadron which took part in the recent naval battle in which the Germans sustained heavy loss and were completely beaten, is a resident of Coulsdon, living at The Rectory when not on active service.'

SPECIALS

At home it was reported that 58 resident tradesmen and City men had enrolled as Special Constables, and a proposal was put forward to raise a company of the Volunteer Civil Force. The Inspector was Mr Walford, of 'Downe Cottage', Hollymeoak Road, and the objective of the specials was to relieve the regular police and do four-hour shifts. Squad drills and concerts were held at St Andrew's Hall, Brighton Road, and there was an Orderly Room at Smitham Council Schools. There were some early promotions among the specials, and their area was extended to Horley – "now the order is being enforced for all motor cars to travel without the glaring headlight, they will have a very busy time". There is also a reference to guarding the railway line from camps at Hooley and Merstham Tunnel when the Liverpool territorials were replaced by the 10th Company of London.

THE WAR EFFORT

A Patriotic Fund for Coulsdon & Purley was set up at an open meeting held at the Congregational Hall, Purley in 1914. Its objective was to organise relief measures, and a committee was formed and resolutions passed. £1200 was raised at the meeting, and the national anthem was sung. The Fund's motto was *He gives twice who gives quickly*.

Two months later under a heading 'Coulsdon preparing to fight the foe' a local newspaper reported the formation of a Shooting & Training Association at St Andrew's Hall. The meeting was presided over by J Saltmarsh and supported by Revd Granville Dickson (Rector), Revd J C Crawford (Chaplain at Cane Hill), Revd Francis Roberts (Vicar of Coulsdon), Revd Harold Chappell (Wesleyan Church minister) etc. The national anthem was sung, with Revd Roberts leading on piano, and Revd Dickson gave a patriotic speech designed to get local men to enlist. In Dickson's own circle of friends, Mr Babington's four sons were serving; as also were Mr Tufnell's two sons and Mr Ellis's only son.

BELGIAN RELIEF

A scheme for a Coulsdon Belgian Home was started in 1914, when A E Bates offered a house for 12 refugees, rent-free. The elected committee was P C Mayhew (treasurer) from The Drive; Mrs H Heasman (secretary) from 'Chimney Cottage', Woodcote Grove Road, and Mrs Gonzales from 'Almeria' in Woodcote Grove Road. The cause was immediately taken up by the Coulsdon Workmen's Club, which promoted a Belgian Refugee Concert at St Andrew's Church Hall. A report in 1916 locates the Coulsdon Belgian Hostel at 'Leenane', Brighton Road, Purley.

In 1915 the Lord Lieutenant of Surrey, Colonel the Hon Henry Cubitt attended the inauguration of the Coulsdon Volunteer Training Corps at its Headquarters at Stoats Nest Farm, where a rifle range had been set up. Another prestigious visitor was Princess Helena, third daughter of Queen Victoria, who opened the YMCA hut in St Andrew's Hall in 1918.

ROLE OF THE CHURCHES

In August 1914 special services were held at St Andrew's Church and the Methodist Church. Doubtless there were others, and there are reports in 1916 of intercession services at St Andrew's where there was a large attendance and at St Aidan's where Father Walsh preached in the morning and Father Roe in the evening. At the Wesleyan Methodist Church in 1918, there was another Intercession Sunday when special music was played, prayers approved by His Majesty offered, and the Roll of Honour read.

FEMALES AT WAR

Early in the war classes for nurses were held in St Andrew's Hall by Doctors Kellett and Ryan. Phyllis Kellett, an 11 year-old daughter of the Coulsdon doctor, managed to obtain 6000 cigarettes for wounded soldiers and she thanked the traders of Coulsdon and Purley. Under a heading CIGARETTES FOR TOMMIES – A LITTLE GIRL'S REWARD, a local newspaper reprinted a letter of thanks from a soldier and her father was to take her to a London hospital to distribute the cigarettes personally.

In 1916 there was yet another concert at St Andrew's Hall, given by many young ladies interested in the Young Helpers' League, to assist the funds of Dr Barnardo's Homes and also for the forces at the front. Later in the same year a note for emancipation was recorded—

LOCAL ENTERPRISE

As evidence of the enterprise shown by Coulsdon tradesmen we see that Mr Fred Cottage, builder and decorator, is now employing women as decorators with success. They wear a most suitable uniform while at work, which looks quite businesslike, and we congratulate our fellow tradesman for his enterprise.

(Above) **Coulsdon Memorial Recreation Ground, photographed in 1949. The canopied memorial in the distance was dedicated on 16 April 1921.** *Photo courtesy of Purley Library.* *(Below)* **The names inscribed on the memorial**

IN THE GREAT WAR 1914-1919

ALMOND, P.J.	FRANKS, L.B.	JEFFERY, S.J.	PIGGOTT, D.T. MC.
BABINGTON, R.V.	FRANKS, R.S.	JOYCE, H.G.	QUIN, F.J.
BARNES, A.	FULLALOVE, G.	KEY, G.W.	RICE, H.C.
BARNES, J.C.	GANE, W.E., MC.	KING, A.E.	ROBINSON, W.S.
BARRELL, H.O.	GARRARD, F.G. MC.	KING, W.J.	ROBINSON, C.L. MM.
BAXTER, F.J.	GIBBS, W.T.	LEACH, A.	RUMBLE, G.H.
BEACH, L.H.F. DS	GRAVES, F.G.	LEE, W.G.	RUSSELL, A.
BECKETT, F.H.	HALLIDAY, E.	LEISTEN, F.W.	SAVAGE, A.J.
BURTON, H.R.	HERRON, F.	LLOYD, F.J.	SHRIMPTON, W.O.
CARVER, H.	HICKMAN, H.F.	LUCAS, H.W.	SMETHURST, C.V.
CHAPMAN, A.E.	HICKS, F.H.	MARVIN, D.	STEWARD, F.J.
CLAYTON, K.H.	HILL, F.J.W.	MARVIN, H.J.	TONKIN, T.
CLEMENTS, C.C.	HIGHGATE, M.W.	McDOUGALL, L.R.	TUCKNOTT, G.C.
COOPER, T.	HODGE, P.	MERRETT, A.E.	TULLEY, J.R.
CORDERY, H.T.	HOOKER, A.C.	MOORE, E.C.	TURNER, J.
CURTIS, A.	IVORY, J.A	NOEL, H.C.N.	VINING, W.
DYKE, W.B.	JENNES, A.	PEELING, A.W.	WOOD, W.A.
FLECKER, H.	JEFFERY, A.S.	PENFOLD, H.	WRIGHT, L.N.
BELL, J.R.C.	CHUTTER, G.P.	PERRY, A.S.	COOPER, C.G.

WOUNDED SOLDIERS AT ASHDOWN PARK

The following description appeared under the above heading in July 1916—

The beautiful grounds surrounding the Ashdown Park Hotel, never looked more charming than on Saturday last when about 20 wounded soldiers from the Purley Hospital were entertained by the visitors at the hotel, and the proprietor, Mr Miller. Situate at the foot of Farthing Down amid beauteous scenery, the gallant heroes of many a fight were highly delighted with the reception accorded them and the entertainment and tea provided, to which the men stationed on guard belonging to the Defence Corps were also included. The well-kept lawns in front of the hotel were marked out for bowls, croquet, tennis and miniature golf and competitions arranged for which prizes were awarded. Here the heroes emulated Drake on the Hoe when the Armada was sighted, and handled golf club and tennis racquet with precision until the time for tea, which was a sumptuous repast in every respect. The good things provided being disposed of, the soldiers were now entertained by a capital concert party to music, song and dance, and the competitive games were then resumed, a most enjoyable afternoon being spent under ideal conditions. Needless to say the warworn heroes were profuse in their thanks to the visitors at the hotel and the proprietor for their great kindness, which they tendered by hearty cheers on leaving the grounds of the establishment.

**The stone and flint memorial cross near St John's Church dedicated on
14 September 1919, before it was repositioned**

Photograph courtesy of Croydon Local Studies Library

THE HEROES

The early enthusiasm to join the forces is evident from the following—

PATRIOTIC COULSDON

Young men and veterans, residents of Coulsdon, are still coming forward and joining the ranks to fight for their King and country and all that they hold near and dear to them. This week among the recruits who have offered their services are Reginald Westover, William King, T Banfield, A Hooker, H Mothers, H Randall, L Wright, Dunkeld, Percy Herrons, Gwyn and Saw...

JOINING THE ARMY

When the history of the war is written the name of Coulsdon will figure largely, considering its size and population, in the honour's list, for the number of men who have joined the army from Coulsdon to fight for their country... Mr Frank Sheldon, late attendant at Cane Hill Asylum, son of Constable Sheldon, has enlisted in the Royal Garrison Artillery, whilst Mr Hubert King and Mr Hellier have joined the 17th Lancers. Mr Cook and Mr T Cole, Coulsdon residents at the Epsom Institution have enlisted this week...

Later in the war, following the unforeseen slaughter, the tone of the newspaper reports is far more solemn—

FALLEN IN THE GREAT BATTLE

It is with the greatest regret that information is coming to hand of the great losses the Empire is sustaining through the loss of the gallant men fighting for all that is dear and among them many Coulsdon men who include Lieut-Quartermaster Addey-Jibb of 6 Edward Road... The gallant soldier, a fine specimen of manhood, had been on active service in France since the war broke out and much sympathy is extended to his friends and family.

KILLED IN ACTION

News arrived at the beginning of the week of the death of Private Jeanes of Edward Road, who has fallen in the defence of his country. Formerly in the employ of Messrs Baines & Son, dairymen, this worthy citizen was called to the colours at 42 years of age and after a short training was drafted to France and had taken part in the campaign since that time. He leaves a widow and two children to mourn his loss.

DEATH

of Private Arthur Savage, 18 Woodman Road who was killed in action during the recent fighting, the news arriving last week. This brave Coulsdon soldier has seen much fighting since war was declared, he having taken part in many severe sections on the French Front...

AMONG THE MISSING

Several Coulsdon lads are recorded among the missing. No news has been received by Mr & Mrs Steward of their son, but hopes are entertained that he is safe, his name not being in the casualty list. We hear that a son of Mr Herron the Coulsdon sweep, is among the missing, and reported a prisoner.

WOUNDED AND GASSED

We regret to hear that Private Baden Lee, son of Mr & Mrs Lee of Chipstead Road, Coulsdon, who only five weeks since went to France, has been wounded and badly gassed and is at present in hospital in England.

The horrors of war were apparent to all, and in the year of the Armistice the local war effort continued with Mr Pigott, a well-known Coulsdon farmer, taking over the 139 acres of Woodcote Park Estate, which he quickly ploughed and sowed with wheat.

**Old Coulsdon War Memorial, in
its present permanent position
fronting Grange Park, close to
St John's Church**

Photographed in 2000

The local newspapers record letters from the front, details of home leave, the wounded and the fallen. The latter included sons of gentlemen such as Ralph Babington from 'The Grange'; shopkeepers such as Ernest Leisten; the heroic scoutmaster from the 1910 Stoats Nest train crash – F H Beckett, the founder of the local troop – and the local policeman, H Penfold.

By January 1916, 379 men had passed through the Coulsdon Recruitment Office, although 114 failed the medical examination, and at the conclusion of the conflict the tragic loss of 41 local men was recorded on the St John's memorial cross and 76 commemorated at Marlpit Lane Memorial Ground.

SOURCES

Coulsdon & Purley Weekly Record 1914-18

BROADBENT, U & LATHAM, R (Eds) (1976) *Coulsdon – Downland Village.* The Bourne Society

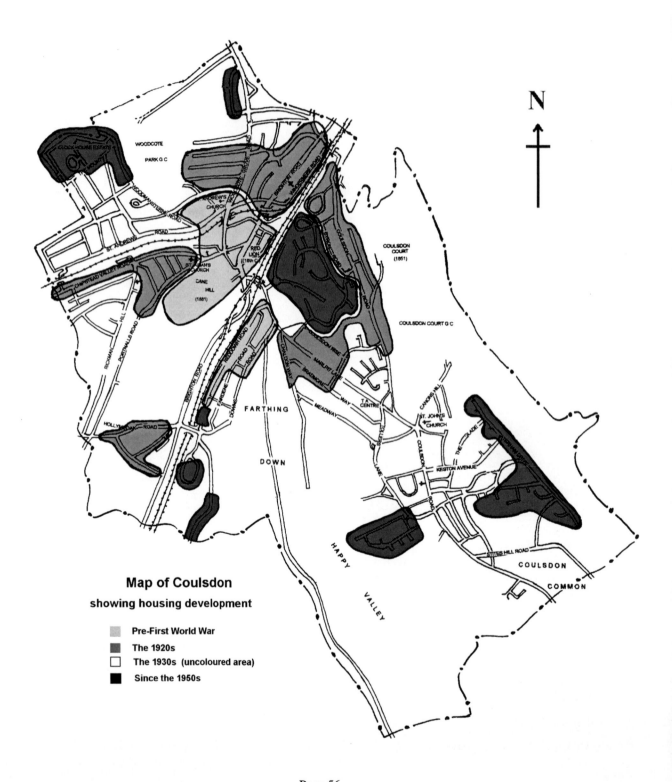

N

Map of Coulsdon

showing housing development

Pre-First World War
The 1920s
The 1930s (uncoloured area)
Since the 1950s

Chapter 9

Urban Development between the Wars

by Ian Scales & Ken Righton

The end of World War I saw what was still a small, largely farming, village saddened by the loss of so many of its sons commemorated on the two memorials, a shocking total when one considers that the population was around 2000 at the time, not counting the patients in Cane Hill Asylum, as it was then called. Families from every quarter had suffered the loss of sons and fathers. Then almost immediately the Spanish 'flu epidemic struck, accounting for more.

Within hours of the last shots of the war a group of 'Comrades of the Great War' met in *The Red Lion* to inaugurate the Comrades' Club and on 4 August 1920 the former St Andrew's Hall was opened by Colonel F de B Young, CMG. It was superseded in 1933 by the present Comrades' Hall and the old hall was given to the South London Harriers as their headquarters.

The official Peace Day in July 1919 was celebrated in traditional fashion by sports for the children in the football field belonging to Marlpit Farm – situated where Marlpit Lane and Chaldon Way now meet. The parade to the sports was headed by the buglers of the Coulsdon Boy Scouts and was followed by tea and an entertainment at which each child received a commemoration mug.

Ever since the building of Cane Hill Asylum in the 1880s there had been two communities – at Smitham Bottom and at the present Old Coulsdon – and this caused some dissent when it came to planning a war memorial. In 1919 a cross made from stone and local flint was dedicated to the fallen of the ecclesiatical parish, near St. John's Church, which had been its hub for 900 years, but the new suburb on Brighton Road had little connection with the hilltop village and wanted its own memorial. Various sites were considered, including one on Farthing Downs and another for a clock tower near *The Red Lion*, but there was little support for them. Finally, 11 acres at the bottom of Marlpit Lane were bought from Squire Byron, who knocked £100 off the purchase price as his donation, and the Memorial Recreation Ground was laid out, the canopied shrine with its Roll of Honour being dedicated on 16 April 1921.

COULSDON EAST & OLD COULSDON

'Homes fit for heroes' were being built all over the country for returning ex-servicemen, and Coulsdon & Purley Urban District Council planned such a housing estate to be located near Stoats Nest Road. Initially Squire Byron, who owned the land, refused to sell it and eventually a compulsory purchase order was needed before Stoats Nest Village could be started in 1919.

The building of Cane Hill Asylum had resulted in much housing and many small shops being built in Woodman Road, Chipstead Valley Road and Lion Green Road. These joined those built nearer Coulsdon North (or Stoats Nest) Station to serve the needs of the hundred and more railway employees and their families in Station Approach, Victoria Road and Edward Road. On the 'other side of the tracks' – literally – upmarket housing in Reddown Road and the more northern ends of Fairdene and Downs Roads followed the opening of Coulsdon South station in 1889. Part of this housing was aimed at the servants needed for the large houses in Reddown and Fairdene Roads as well as for more senior servants from Coulsdon Court.

On 30 April 1921 Edmund Byron, the last squire to live in Coulsdon, died in his 78th year after nearly 60 years of lording it over his tenant farmers and estate workers. In his time the world had changed. His country gentleman's estate was being encroached upon by the tide of London and the pressures of development made it more and more difficult to maintain a farming community in such a place. His son Cecil having died in 1911, Edmund instructed in his Will that the manor be sold. In 1922, Messrs Ellis and Farebrother put the estate up for sale in lots and one by one the farms on the hill were given over to suburban housing. Bradmore Farm and Tollers Farms became riding schools for the new inhabitants and the parkland surrounding Coulsdon Court was bought by the Urban District Council and developed in 1926 into an 18-hole municipal golf course, Coulsdon Court house being used for its clubrooms. Along with this purchase came the manorial rights and so the UDC became Lord of the Manor of Coulsdon, to be succeeded in 1965 by the London Borough of Croydon.

Development of the Byron land started round the old 'skeleton' of existing roads – Coulsdon Road, Hartley Down and Marlpit Lane. This last, a 12-foot wide rough track with only Marlpit Farm along it – there since 1878 – was widened and metalled and the first houses appeared towards the end of the 1920s. It had been a favourite run for both cyclists and early motorists, providing a challenge either to stay in the seat when descending, or to rush up in the least possible time while crashing through the gears.

Aerial photograph looking towards Old Coulsdon, Marlpit Lane to centre and Chaldon Way running to right. Photo by Surrey Flying Services, 1929. Courtesy of Purley Library.

Chaldon Way, originally intended to run right through Happy Valley to the medieval village of Chaldon, joined Marlpit Lane at the bottom of the hill, and Coulsdon Rise on the other side of the lane saw their first houses at the same time. Among the first of the new roads on the north side of the hill off Coulsdon Road, was Byron Avenue, keeping the name of the squire's family to remind future generations of a century and a half of history.

Gradually ancient tracks and fields became built-up roads of detached and semi-detached houses and bungalows, so that by the end of the 1920s Tollers Lane, Bradmore Way, Canon's Hill, Petersfield Crescent, Hillars Heath Road and Cearn Way were in the process of swallowing the farmland of the original Byron estates, joining the earlier development of Reddown, Fairdene and Downs Roads.

URBAN DEVELOPMENT BETWEEN THE WARS

Canon's Hill – a bridleway being turned into a road – 1933

Photograph courtesy of Croydon Local Studies Library

Despite the depression that lasted through much of the 1930s, development in Old Coulsdon proceeded apace, the largest estate being that of the Tudor Village, so named from the half-timbered style of the houses and shops. Coulsdon Road south of St John's Church, Court Avenue, Keston Avenue, The Crossways, Tollers Lane and Placehouse Lane formed the major part, along with Taunton Lane. Style varied, though the external timbers were universally featured, but the depression caused a rethink in the matter of costs and the houses were generally smaller than those built in the 1920s. Semi-detached houses were to sell for 'not less than £600' and detached versions for 'not less than £800'. Prices like these sound absurd these days, although £400 was a likely price for a terraced house in Chipstead Valley Road at around the same time. Today the semis sell for more than 200 times as much as they did when new. Mead Way, leading off Chaldon Way and up the hill to Placehouse Lane, was built at this time, cutting its way through Shunaway Plantation. During construction there was an archaeological discovery of a bronze-founder's hoard, comprising five socketed and looped bronze axes, which can now be seen in Guildford Museum.

In 1937 the Green Belt Scheme stopped further planned developments around the hill, including an estate between Mead Way and Chaldon Way, where concrete roads, sewers and an electricity sub-station were laid down and it might have been completed had not war come in 1939. Today, secondary growth of ash, sycamore and elder trees have blotted out nearly all traces of the scheme, but the entry roads are still visible as gaps between the otherwise continuous housing plots. Chaldon Way stops abruptly in its march along Happy Valley, leaving that beautiful area available to walkers and searchers for many rare chalk downland plants. Similarly, Canon's Hill was prevented from being developed through the woods leading to Old Lodge Lane and another road from the bottom of Caterham Drive to a point near *The Wattenden Arms* public house in Old Lodge Lane was never started, or even named.

Another estate begun in the early 1930s was very different in style to those already described – the Coulsdon Vale Estate off Woodplace Lane. This comprised two roads – The Netherlands and Wilhelmina Avenue – forming a 'Modern Dutch Garden Village', as it was described by its Dutch architect Wouter Hamdorff, who used continental-sized bricks imported from Holland in construction. These, together with the continental design of the houses, produced a very attractive alternative to the mock Tudor style used elsewhere, so despite their comparatively high prices (£995 to £1185) they sold well. Construction stopped in 1937 and the estate was not finished until after World War II. Wouter Hamdorff had returned to his native land, and is believed to have been killed during the terrible bombing raid on Rotterdam in 1940.

COULSDON WEST

Apart from the building associated with Cane Hill, another early development should be mentioned – the south side of Bramley Avenue, Julien Road and Southwood Avenue had been built in the time of Edward VII, taking advantage of the superb views across the valley to Farthing Downs and the farms in Old Coulsdon.

Looking eastwards across Coulsdon from Bramley Avenue

The houses 0n the right are in Julien Road and the school buildings in Malcolm Road can be seen between the houses in Woodmansterne Road. 1912

Coulsdon from Bramley Avenue.

Other major areas on the west side of Brighton Road were developed during the 1920s and early 1930s. That between Brighton Road and Woodcote Grove Road was built to take advantage of the train services to London from the close-by Smitham and Coulsdon North stations, together with the proximity of the rapidly growing shopping centre in Brighton Road. It contains many fine houses, nearly all detached and placed so that it is impossible to overlook, or be overlooked by, neighbours. Five cul-de-sacs ensured a special privacy, while The Wend, The Ridge, The Grove, The Drive and South Drive are all curved for the same reason. Extensive growth of shrubs and trees in the intervening 60 or 70 years have added to this attraction. It is worth noting that, before housing was developed on this hill, Smitham Downs was almost bare of trees – a classic example of chalk downland.

Coulsdon. View from the Grove.

View looking north-east across Coulsdon, with Reedham Orphanage in the distance. *c*.1912

The land to the west of Woodcote Grove Road was built on at the same time, taking advantage of its proximity to Woodcote Park Golf Club. Houses convenient for the golfing fraternity were built in The Chase, Warwick Road and Howard Road in the 1920s, with Grove Wood Hill and the north side of Bramley Avenue joining them in the 1930s.

A notable resident, at 40 Warwick Road, was Benjamin Clapp, chief engineer to John Logie Baird. Between them they were developing television in the 1920s, and taking advantage of the unobstructed views from the hill. Mr Clapp installed a tall aerial in his garden, from which in 1928 the very first television transmission was made across the Atlantic to New York .

Two other areas originally developed to the west of Brighton Road in the 1920s should be mentioned – first Starrock Road, Woodfield Hill and Hollymeoak Road, which were built on roads released for development by Portnalls Farm. The name 'Hollymeoak' was originally 'Hollyme Oak' – 'holm oak' – a species of oak native to the Mediterranean region .

Secondly, Portnalls Road, Portnalls Rise, Vincent Road, Sherwood Road and Coniston Road were added along the south side of Chipstead Valley Road, which was also developed in the 1920s.

A further two dozen roads were laid out and completed on the west side of Coulsdon before World War II stopped everything for a decade and more. Both sides of the west end of Chipstead Valley Road and Woodmansterne station were built during the 1930s. From The Mount and Fryston Avenue in the north to Rickman Hill in the south, terraces and semi-detached houses sprang up to meet the ever increasing need to house people away from the smoke of London and Croydon, while at the same time allowing fast access by railway to these centres.

All this housing demanded servicing in the form of schools, churches, libraries, clubs, meeting halls and shops. Between the wars there existed St John's school, now known as Bradmore Green Primary School. It had served the farming community since 1845, when Squire Thomas Byron III gave the land where it now stands. Rebuilt in 1888, it was bursting at the seams by the 1920s and 1930s trying to educate the children from the new developments. In 1936 an additional primary school was built in Keston Avenue. Smitham School had been built in the 1880s to serve the houses round Cane Hill and Chipstead Valley Road and a number of smaller schools in both communities served the needs of those families able to pay for private education.

It was 1933 before Coulsdon could boast a secondary school. Prior to that, Purley had both Boys' and Girls' Grammar Schools, but both were moved to Old Coulsdon in the decade before World War II.

St John's Church of England had existed for over 900 years; the Methodist Church on Brighton Road had been built before World War I, and St Aidan's in Woodcote Grove Road had existed since the early part of the century, serving the Roman Catholic residents, to be joined by St Mary Help of Christians in Old Coulsdon. St Andrew's and St Francis' churches (C of E) served their communities to the west. In the 20 years between the world wars Coulsdon had changed considerably from the small farming village on the hill, the large hospital and the community in Smitham Bottom to a suburb of some 12,000 souls.

ROAD NAMES

The oldest roads in Coulsdon are Brighton Road, Chipstead Valley Road, Coulsdon Road, Marlpit Lane, Tollers Lane and Taunton Lane. All other roads have been built up round these at various times during the last 120 years.

Coulsdon Road at one time was known as Coulsdon Street, and the handful of houses in the old village of 1921 had no gas, electricity or street lighting. Piped water had not arrived except to Coulsdon Court, from which it was extended to three standpipes in the back yards of Nos. 1-6 Coulsdon Street. Other people – in the better-off houses – had their own wells; the rest used the ponds that were scattered across the top of the hill at Bradmore Green, Placehouse Farm, Lacey Green and The Sisters Pond near *The Fox*.

As the village expanded from the 1920s , following sale of the land for development, roads were given names that often related to the field they were built over, the farm they occupied, or else after local personalities or the names of the builder's family. A selection of road names with their derivations follows—

Admiral's Walk	From Admiral Sir William Goodenough, hero of World War I who lived in Parson's Pightle and whose grave is in St John's churchyard.
Benham Close	After John de Benham, an abbot of Chertsey Abbey, which administered the manor from 675 AD to 1536.
Bishop's Close	Named in keeping with the ecclesiastical name of Canon's Hill, next to St John's church.
Bradmore Way	Named after Bradmore Green and Bradmore Farm, the traditional home of the Colgrime family. Bainbridge's map of 1785 refers to both 'Bradmore' and 'Bradmoor' when naming fields.
Byron Avenue	After Squire Edmund Byron who had owned the land on which Stoats Nest Village was built. Named to appease him for having had the land taken from him by compulsory purchase in order to build houses for servicemen returning from World War I.
Byron Place Estate	Built on the site of the Purley High School for Girls, demolished in 1992. The road names, all of famous poets, are a reminder of the literary aspirations of the Girls' School—
	Betjeman Close, Larkin Close, Rosetti Gardens, Shelley Close.
Canon's Hill	Named in honour of Canon Hubert Granville Dickson, Rector of St John's church for 33 years. He used the footpath (as it was then) when walking between church and his rectory in Hayes Lane.
Carew Close	After the Carew family, lords of the manor after Henry VIII dissolved the monasteries.
Cearn Way	Charles Cearn bought Coulsdon Court and its park from the estate of Edmund Byron, and among the roads he developed was Cearn Way, which used to be the tradesmen's entrance to the Court.
Cherry Tree Court	Built in the grounds of Cherry Tree Cottage, 210 Coulsdon Road, which is a half-timbered house dating from 1639 which has had a variety of uses down the years: *Cherry Tree Inn* (1880), then the village shop, post office, butcher's shop, before returning to private occupation. The Cottage was a fire and ambulance call point during World War II.
Chipstead Valley Road	Originally called Chipstead Road – the way to Reigate via High Road, Chipstead.
Coulsdon Road	Main road from Brighton Road *via* Stoats Nest Road, to the borders of Caterham.
Coulsdon Court Road	The main drive leading to Coulsdon Court, since 1993 called Coulsdon Manor Hotel when it was bought by the Marston Hotel group.
Court Avenue	Not far from the medieval Coulsdon Court house, now known as The Grange. Court Avenue bisects South Field, one of the four original Saxon strip fields in the 8th century.
Crossways	So named as it joined the parallel original roads of Coulsdon Road and Tollers Lane. Its site until the 19th century was the local brickfield which produced the bricks to build Coulsdon Court in the 1850s.
Dean's Walk	Like Bishop's Close off Canon's Hill, named to retain the ecclesiastical connection.

**Men at work in
Coulsdon Road in
1936**

*Photograph courtesy
of Croydon Local
Studies Library*

**Downs Road. When it
was built it was named
Fanfare Road, and the
name changed in 1912**

**Court Avenue,
photographed in 2000**

**This was one of the
first Tudor Estate roads
to be built**

A HISTORY OF COULSDON

Downs Road
Running alongside Farthing Downs, it was built at the beginning of the 20th century when it was called Fanfare Road, presumably to mark the accession of King Edward VII. It became Downs Road in 1912.

Dunstan Road
Never developed, running between Downs Road and Fairdene Road. The name also appears on a terrace of houses built to accommodate staff of Cane Hill Asylum and appears as a field name on Cane Hill in the 18th century.

Drive Road
Derived from the 'driftway', meaning a farm track, leading to Tollers Farm. Beyond the farm where it reaches open land above Happy Valley it has no name.

Ellis Close
Ellis Road
Named after F H B Ellis, historian and chairman of Coulsdon & Purley Urban District Council. He photographed the area extensively, creating a remarkable record of its 20th century development.

Fairdene Road
Fairdene was at one time the name of Farthing Downs. The road is named since it runs alongside the Downs.

Forge Avenue
The village blacksmith's forge stood nearby until the 1930s.

Fox Lane
Named after *The Fox* public house close by on Coulsdon Common.

The Glade
After the woodland glade through which it was built in the 1930s.

Goodenough Close
Goodenough Way
After Admiral Sir William Goodenough, who lived close by in Parson's Pightle. (see Admiral's Walk above).

Hartley Down
Hartley Hill
Hartley Old Road
Hartley Way
Hartley Farm covered this area. Hartley Farm house stood on the site now occupied by Coulsdon Court before Squire Byron demolished it to replace it with his house in 1850. New Hartley Farmhouse was then built between Hartley Down and Hartley Hill and was a busy dairy farm until 1921. Now a private house, it was ARP Wardens' Post No. 15 during World War II.

Hillars Heath Road
Named after a field on 18th century maps.

Inwood Avenue
Named after the wood through which The Glade runs. Old references called it Nymmwood, changing to Ninwood and finally Inwood. In 1805 it was recorded as Linne Wood.

Kerrill Avenue
Named for the Kerrill family who owned the land in 1783. Lacey Green was once known as Kerrill's Green because it was on their land.

Lacey Avenue
Lacey Drive
Lacey Green
After the landowner Henry Lacy in 1296, a famous family from Lassy in Normandy. The Lacie family (the spelling referred to in 1333 in Edward III's reign) were joint tenants of Placehouse Farm (see Placehouse Lane) with the Salmon family. In 1548 the whole area was called Lacyland. The 'e' in the current spelling was added during the 20th century.

Lion Green Road
Named after the green opposite *The Red Lion* public house.

Marlpit Lane
Pits dug for marl – a calcareous clay – were a feature of farmland. The marl was added as a valuable fertiliser to the poor chalky soil of the district. The marl pit was in the Marl Field and the road alongside it was called Marling Pit Hill. The name was changed to Chalk Pit Field by 1783, a misnomer which was corrected in the late 19th century to its present name. The chalk quarry was not worked until the 1860s, when its chalk was limed for cement and the flints as a source of silica. The quarry site is now an industrial estate.

Moorsom Way
The maiden name of the wife of the local landowner and developer, Oscar Wilson Roberts, who built properties in Downs Road and the surrounding area. He owned Hooley House, later called Ashdown Park, which was demolished in the 1970s.

URBAN DEVELOPMENT BETWEEN THE WARS

The Netherlands Part of the 'Dutch Village', so called because a Dutch building firm imported Dutch workers to build the houses there with imported Dutch bricks.

Old Fox Close Named after *The Fox* public house nearby.

Petersfield Crescent After a field name 'Old Peter's Three Score Acres' shown on the Thomas Bainbridge Map of 1785.

Portnalls Road The road leading from the valley to Portnalls Farm, which, together with Portnalls Oaks, a small wood roughly where Smitham School is now located, is named after John Portenhale, the owner in 1362.

Reddown Road The name of a field there, shown in Messeder's Fieldbook, 1762.

Redlands There was a field called Redlam Bottom on this site 200 years ago.

Rickman Hill From John Ruckenham, constable of Wallington Hundred, one of four Coulsdon men known to have taken part in Jack Cade's Peasants' Revolt of 1450.

Rogers Close Off Caterham Drive; named after Roger Plater, son of the builder.

Stanley Close Sir John Stanley owned a large amount of land in the area during the 18th century.

Stoats Nest Road Named after Stoats Nest Farm through which it ran. The farm was demolished after World War I though some buildings remained until the 1920s. Stoats Nest Road was originally called Larkin Lane.

Stoneyfield Road On the site of the field so-named in Messeder's Fieldbook of 1762.

Taunton Lane Leading to Taunton Farm, named after the owners of the sub-manor of Taunton, the de Tauntons. In 1234 the sub-manor was given to the 'Hospital of St Thomas the Martyr of Acre' who retained it until the Dissolution of the Monasteries in 1536.

Tollers Lane After Robert Toller who owned the farm here in 1332. The area was referred to as 'Tollersland' in 1432.

Demonstration Poultry Farm in Waddington Avenue in the 1930s

The house remains

Waddington Avenue A corruption of 'Watendone', the name of the village mentioned with Coulsdon in Domesday Book but which has long-since been lost, possibly as a result of the Black Death in the 14th century.

Woodplace Lane Road leading to Woodplace Farm.

Lawson Hunter, who came to
Coulsdon when he was five
years old

**Two of Coulsdon's senior
citizens whose memories
paint a colourful picture of
Coulsdon life over many
years**

Rosie Watts, née Huggett, born in
Coulsdon during World War I

Chapter 10

Reminiscences

In the course of research for the village history, it was a pleasure to speak to some of the village's older residents and record some of their memories. Mr Lawson Hunter came to Coulsdon in 1913 when he was 5 years old. Mrs Rosie Watts, born in 1917, has contributed several articles to the Society's **Bulletins** and *Local History Records,* and a short excerpt is included here. The extract from Miss Hilary Greenwood's reminiscences covers the late 1930s.

Conversation with Lawson Hunter

Lawson Walton Hunter was born in Twickenham in 1908 where he remembers watching the Kaiser in a carriage on a visit to the exiled King Emanuel of Portugal. He also remembers the embryo rugby ground there and falling out of a bedroom window, landing on his bottom which soon received a smack! His father was a barrister's clerk in London chambers, whose clients included Sir John Lawson Walton, the Attorney-General. His brothers and sisters were Marjorie, Dennis and Maisie but unfortunately Maisie died of TB. She had been in the choir at St John's Old Coulsdon and is buried in the family vault there. There is a memorial plate near the war memorial.

The family came to Coulsdon in 1913 where they rented 44 Reddown Road, complete with the Bourne at the bottom of the garden, before moving opposite to No. 31. In those days the houses finished at Moorsom Way, and Mr Hunter recalls the Fairdene Lawn Tennis Club nearby and the nine-hole golf course of Ashdown Park.

The young Lawson went to Fairdene Kindergarten in Reddown Road, where he was taught by Miss James, but when his father was called up as a private in 1914 he was obliged to transfer to Bradmore Green. The headmistress there was Miss Churchill, and her young pupil remembers weeding the garden path between the school and schoolhouse, for which he received 2d. Father returned safely from the Cycling Corps and a proud son retains his father's Identity card.

Marlpit Lane was a muddy track in winter and Keeble's Farm its only building, where milk was obtained. A junior Keeble took Lawson to Hartley Farm for tea in a horse-drawn milk cart. Bread was sold from Pillings' bakers, Brighton Road near The Avenue, where there was always a long queue. The delivery van once went past Coulsdon South Station when the bread tumbled out but was put back!

Lawson's education continued at Purley County Grammar School which was then situated in Godstone Road. The fees were £2.10s.0d per term and R B Wight was the headmaster until 1920, when he was succeeded by Mr Mitchell. The young student was obliged to visit the head's study because a boy had scribbled on his book, but full of apprehension he decided instead to run all the way home. Journeys to school were normally by a two-carriage train pulled by a steam engine from Coulsdon North to Purley. On one occasion a conker was thrown into the driver's cab but the wrong boy was blamed. Mr Hunter senior was called on to ensure that justice prevailed.

Other school memories include Mr Bachelor, the science master, inflicting an electric shock on the pupils with a Wimshurst machine and being quizzed by Mr Hill (mathematics) about his unusual christian name, which resulted in a nickname of Billy. Mr Hunter's hearing handicap made lessons difficult but he excelled at English. He recalls walking to the school's sports field near Kenley station, and the formation of the Old Boys' Rugby Football Club which had E J Austin as its first captain. Lawson's recollections include going to the cinema in Malcolm Road, travelling with his mother to Surrey Street, Croydon on the bus for 4d, and walking along Farthing Downs to Chaldon and *The Spotted Cow* at Warwick Wold.

As a young man Lawson was good at lawn tennis and played at Mr Lovering's Fairdene Club before it was built on. He was also a keen cyclist, and would ride to Brighton and Seaford College to see his brother. On one occasion when cycling to Purley, Mr Cearn's car fell on him in Reddown Road and the fire brigade was obliged to release him and he was taken to hospital. To everyone's surprise Lawson cycled along the road the next day! One of Mr Cearn's employees was Mr Hunt from 15 Reddown Road; in those days it was Miss Phyllis Hunt who attracted Lawson's attention.

Young Hunter was a boy scout, and remembers the hut in the woods at the top of Moorsom Way and watching soldiers digging trenches on the downs. The scouts visited Pound Cottage, where mapmaking and map reading were taught by F H B Ellis, a big man and Chairman of the Council – he taught them the meaning of HE (horizontal equivalent) and VI (vertical interval) when drawing maps of the district. Another local celebrity was Canon Dickson, who confirmed the young Hunter and gave him a treasured book, inscribed 'Lawson Walton Hunter from his sincere friend H Granville Dickson, Rector of Coulsdon 23 March 1924'.

Father resumed his career after the war and became a judge's clerk, which gave him the opportunity to arrange a seven year apprenticeship for his son with earnings of 5s. weekly. The 16 year old apprentice was obliged to attend Geo Barber & Son (legal printers) in Cursitor Street and he remembers dashing off to Coulsdon South Station – he could see the railway signal from his home in Reddown Road. At work he had to hand-set statements for plaintiffs and defendants as well as affidavits but he later operated a monotype machine with punch holes in the paper. Later Lawson lodged at Tonbridge where he worked for Truscott's printers.

Soon after the death of his mother, Lawson met his future wife on board *The Strathavon* in 1939. The cruise ended dramatically when the ship returned, being the last one out of the Adriatic before the war. During World War II, Lawson served in the Home Guard as a sentry despite his hearing difficulties, and worked in munitions in a factory on Purley Way. This led to work on the first De Havilland Comet aeroplane with a precision engineering company in Mitcham.

When the war ended, Lawson and Ella married in 1946 and bought the family home in Winifred Road for £1,250. No mortgage was required and a car was purchased out of some money made on shares.

Lawson was skilled at munitions turning and grinding and continued in precision engineering until returning to the print industry with Eyre & Spottiswoode and later to the Jupiter Press on Purley Way, where he became a reader and the union's father of the chapel. On retirement he embarked with his wife on a world cruise for three months.

In recent years Lawson Hunter has supported local events and is remembered for his energetic involvement with Bourne Society tours and for editing the Society's journals between 1987 and 1995.

Memories of Smitham Bottom – by Rosie Watts *née* Huggett

We lived at 45 Woodman Road and I first went to school at Smitham in 1921 when I was five years old. My mother took me to see the headmistress, Miss Read, and then after putting my name in the register Miss Read took me to my classroom. I was very lucky then because the teacher was Mrs Gates who happened to live near me in Woodman Road, so it was nice that my first teacher was someone I knew.

The first thing I noticed in the classroom was a lovely open fire with a big fire guard round it, and in the fireplace were about four medicine bottles full of milk, put there to keep warm; I later learned that they were for the children who lived too far away to go home at dinner time, so they were allowed to bring sandwiches. I also noticed a cane hanging by the blackboard but this did not worry me very much as I knew if I behaved myself I would be OK. My mother also had one hanging on a picture at home in the kitchen but I never remember her or my father using it; it was there to let me and my brothers know we had to behave ourselves at the dinner table and it really did work, as we never moved from the table until the meal was over and we were given permission to leave.

Sometimes when we came out of school in the afternoons there would be a man standing with a hand cart outside. He would tell the children to go home and ask their mothers for some rags and he would give them a balloon or goldfish. He did not come very often because not many mothers had rags to give away.

There has always been a butcher's shop in Chipstead Valley Road opposite the school. When I was small the butcher's name was Ernie Hawkins. It was quite exciting on a Monday when the farmers brought their cattle to be slaughtered. They stopped their carts in Chipstead Valley Road and the animals were unloaded and driven down the alley to the slaughterhouse which was at the back of the shop. Sometimes a lively bullock or sheep would escape and go tearing down the road towards *The Red Lion*. From the safety of the school railings the children would thoroughly enjoy this excitement.

Next to the alley was a little shop (I think it is an estate agent's now) which sold groceries. It was owned by Granny Hawkins, mother of the butcher. She was very clever at making ointment and medicines from herbs. It was cheaper to go to her for a bottle of medicine or ointment than to have the doctor; you only had him if you were too ill to get up and he charged half-a-crown a visit, which was a lot of money then. Unfortunately nearly all the children caught measles, whooping cough, scarlet fever, diphtheria and chicken pox because there were no vaccinations against these diseases. The only thing we had then was vaccination against smallpox, usually done when you were a baby, but if you were older when it was done you had a scarlet piece of ribbon tied round your arm to let other people know to be careful and not bang your arm. All cases of scarlet fever and diphtheria were taken by 'Fever Ambulance' to the isolation hospital in Beddington. I was there for three months with diphtheria. It would have been a lot different if we had had the antibiotics that are available today.

One day when I got home from school my dad told me to go round and collect as many of my friends as I could and take them to the top of Woodman Road. In those days there were no houses built at that end of the road, it was just a big grassy bank which overlooked Chipstead Valley Road. Dad made us all line up along the top of the bank and told us to look towards Chipstead railway station. After a while a great big silver object came floating up the valley towards us; it was a beautiful thing, so graceful, but the thing that struck me most was the quiet purring sound of its engines. I think it was the *Graf Zeppelin* and because Dad was a policeman he had been told it would be coming over Coulsdon. I last saw it disappearing towards Purley and I never knew where it went after that.

About twice a year a *Day's Fair* came to Coulsdon. It pitched its caravans, tents, roundabouts and swings on the piece of ground where St Aidan's church now stands. The children from the fair always came to school for the week they were here. We always had a half holiday on Empire Day. We would have a short lesson about the empire, draw a union jack with crayons, sing *God Save the King* and then go home for the rest of the day.

We also had a holiday on Derby Day because such a lot of traffic came through Coulsdon and along Chipstead Valley Road on its way to Epsom. It was thought to be too dangerous for us to be out on the roads. On a busy day my father would sometimes be on point-duty where the traffic lights are now, where Woodcote Grove Road crosses Chipstead Valley Road. There were no traffic lights there then, just a very tall 'stink pipe' in the middle of the cross-roads. The 'stink pipe' has disappeared (so where does the 'stink' go now?). The Derby Day traffic consisted of horses and carts, motor cars, buses and charabancs. In the evening when they were all returning the big boys ran behind the vehicles shouting 'throw out your mouldy coppers'. If the people from the races were in a good mood and had won some money on the horses, they would throw a handful of coppers and the boys all scrambled for them.

A couple of weeks before the Derby it would be a different kind of traffic trekking along towards Epsom – gypsy caravans. In those days the gypsies lived in colourful wooden vans pulled by horses and usually one or two dogs tied to the back of the vans. I am sure these dogs 'came into their own' when they reached Bunny Hill!

The gypsy women would come calling on the houses selling wooden clothes pegs, paper flowers and sprigs of white heather for luck.

The first *Red Lion* I can remember was just a village pub, then in the late 1920s it was rebuilt and made modern with a large ballroom upstairs. It was great to go to a dance at *The Red Lion*, and I was there the night the Crystal Palace burned. Someone came into the dance and said there was a big fire out Croydon way, so we all trooped out and stood in Brighton Road looking towards Croydon where the sky was all red. A bus driver told us the Palace was on fire, so we ran back to get our coats and caught a bus to Purley where we changed to a tram that took us as near as possible to the fire. It was a terrible sight – no one had ever seen such a fire before (it was before the Blitz).

The first time music rang out over the village was when Woolworth's and its neighbouring shops were being built. Before that there were houses all along Chipstead Valley Road with sub-basements facing the footpath; I used to walk along there when it was dark and I could see into the lighted rooms. The music came from the bricklayer on the site, who used to sing as he worked. He had a beautiful and powerful voice which was lovely to hear. I learned later that he had been head choir boy at Wrexham Parish Church and he had come to London to work. He liked Coulsdon so much he had made it his home. Although I had heard him singing it was several years later before we met and eventually married, and then Coulsdon was always home to us.

Reminiscences from the late 1930s – by Hilary Greenwood

We moved to Old Coulsdon from South Croydon in 1936. My mother had seen the house from Coulsdon Court Golf Course. She must have been playing in a match on that day and saw the house, only recently built on Canon's Hill, from the green, since there were no other houses to obscure the view at that time. She persuaded my father that it was the house for us.

The builder was a Mr Pink. He was appropriately named. His round pink face was always surmounted by a bowler hat and he sported a neat white goatee beard. He specialised in building houses with brick and flint exteriors in an attractive style. He also bought wood and panelling from old houses for his interiors. Our staircase and the panelling in the hall and dining room were reputedly from Lord Chesterfield's house. Unfortunately Mr Pink was not so successful when it came to ceilings. After we had moved in, they frequently fell down and all was covered in a cloud of dust and plaster. Apparently his workmen did not get the mixture right.

In those days it was the custom for ladies to welcome newcomers by an exchange of visiting cards. The ladies of the village called to leave a card and my mother returned the calls by leaving hers at their homes. Next she would be invited to tea to meet them. She came back with amusing stories after each visit. Mrs Richardson at The Grange boasted that she had two staircases. My mother thought this an unnecessary statement and rather vulgar! The vicarage was gloomy and she thought the vicar's wife boring. The lady who lived in the house behind the duck pond had bright blue paintwork. My mother decided that as her son was the borough architect, he must have chosen the paint for the house since the doors of the village hall were the same colour. Lady Goodenough, the widow of Admiral Goodenough, was a sweet old lady who wore large hats and lived at Parson's Pightle.

Canon's Hill was only a made-up road as far as The Grange in those days. The rest, which ran down to Old Lodge Lane, was full of potholes that had to be negotiated in wet weather. Residents came out and filled them in now and again. On the whole nobody minded, as it reduced the traffic, and no one wanted to pay road charges. Our dogs sat in the road and any vehicle had to go round them as they refused to budge. Milk was delivered by horse-drawn cart by Curtis'. Errand boys came on bicycles, after one had ordered supplies by telephone from local shops.

REMINISCENCES

Since we were surrounded by fields and woods, it was an ideal place to roam. From our house, I would jump over the fence, cross the field and go down through the wood to a grassy bank covered in primroses, cowslips and violets in spring. From this slope one looked down onto a track called Caterham Drive at the bottom forming a valley. On the far side, we crossed Old Lodge Lane and went up to Kenley Airfield. Gradually over the years, houses began to be built – at first in The Glade.

My father worked in Westminster. My mother drove him to the station and collected him in the evening. In the beginning I think this station was Reedham but later he went from Coulsdon South, and I remember when we went to collect him at ten past six as the evenings drew in, watching the porter light the gas lamps on the platform.

Father became involved in village affairs when he joined the Residents' Association. He worked very hard for the RA, helping to get a second bus route for us, running through Coulsdon and up to *The Tudor Rose,* which he then used to get to the station. He met Mr Littlechild, who became chairman of the Coulsdon & Purley Council, there.

Our household consisted of my parents, my little brother, our nanny and a cook-general who had been with us in Croydon. I went to Eothen School in Caterham. Another child, living in Marlpit Lane, and I went on the 409 bus. Sometimes we walked up Caterham Hill on the way back, to save a penny on the fare and buy sweets. This was stopped when my father bought a packet of bus tickets which we had to use each day.

At school our Director of Music was Imogen Holst. She had a kind and gentle disposition and brought out the best in the children, both in singing and orchestral playing. The highlight was when she brought Vaughan Williams to an end-of-term concert. As I was the youngest in the senior school, I was chosen to present a posy of flowers. I remember him as a very large old man, but that is all. Many years later I came to know his widow.

We had no television, and relied very much on the wireless for entertainment. A classmate, who lived in Kingswood had one of the first television sets. Several children were invited to watch the boat race and stay to lunch. I felt very grown up and wore my best clothes for the occasion. It was most exciting.

Our next-door neighbour, Mrs Lacey, had a refrigerator before we did. We had small earthenware bowls to put milk bottles in, which were filled with cold water and then an earthenware cone was placed over the top which absorbed the cold water. Beans were salted for the winter and eggs kept in a huge crock with isinglass to preserve them. There was much bottling of fruit and jam making too. It is difficult to imagine that plastic did not exist! Wrapping was paper of different sorts, colours and thicknesses. Bakelite was also much in vogue. The gramophone – *His Master's Voice* – was a wind-up one and used needles which were afterwards put amongst the hydrangeas to make them turn blue!

In the winter I went with a friend to Purley Ice Rink and had skating lessons. I wanted white boots and was disconsolate when I got a pair of brown ones for my birthday. My mother said it was nonsense for a little girl who could not skate properly to have white boots. I never achieved the white ones because the war came.

Sometimes we went to the cinema if there was a suitable film for children. We were mad about Shirley Temple and I had a Shirley Temple doll with real blonde curls. Then there were the Walt Disney cartoon films – *Snow White and the Seven Dwarfs* etc. My father took me to *The Classic* at South Croydon – known as the Flea Pit – to see *Alice in Wonderland.*

In 1937 we celebrated the coronation by putting out bunting and flags. Everyone decorated their homes. We had to wait for the Pathé News film to come to the cinema before seeing the ceremony and processions.

Soon rejoicing was over and the talk was of war. We were issued with gas masks, which were kept in cardboard boxes and slung over the back of our classroom chairs. We had frequent practice in wearing them and going to the Anderson shelters in the grounds. There was general anxiety, but it was only on the day that Germany marched into Poland, told to me by Nanny when she came into my bedroom, that I felt real terror.

The day war was declared was a sunny one. I was playing in the front garden with a friend from up the road. My mother called us in and my grandmother came across to hear Mr Chamberlain speak to the nation. When the broadcast was over we went out again to play. No one said anything – suddenly the sirens went to signal an air raid. My playmate's father came running down the road and made her run home. We gathered once again in the drawing room, believing our end had come. My mother gave my grandmother a pile of peas to shell for lunch, to steady her nerves. She sat on the sofa with the colander on her lap, her hands shaking. Nothing happened; we heard the all clear and later found that it had been a false alarm.

From that day onwards our lives changed completely. My father was informed by letter that we were living within a danger zone which would be under military surveillance, because of the proximity to Kenley Airfield, which was to become a fighter station. Families were advised to evacuate. We went to Hope Cove east of Plymouth and I was away for the duration of the war.

Chapter 11

World War II

by Jean Emery & Margaret Davison

On Sunday 3 September 1939, the Prime Minister, Neville Chamberlain, broadcast to the nation from Downing Street – Britain was at war with Germany. All over the country sirens sounded their first air-raid warnings shortly after the broadcast ended. It was a false alarm. Gas masks had been issued, identity cards and ration books were printed, and the black-out was strictly enforced.

The Surrey Mirror told how a well-known Coulsdon resident 'holding an important post in the Auxiliary Fire Service', was driving his car along Brighton Road during a thunderstorm. There came a vivid flash of lightning and, to his astonishment, he saw two elephants in front of him. The driver, a teetotaller, discovered that the animals were being evacuated from London and were being led by a man with a dimmed light!

By the spring of 1940 Anderson shelters were provided free to most householders, and were erected in gardens, the ground space required – with earth banked over them – being 14 ft by 12 ft, 4 ft deep and situated at least 6 ft from the nearest wall of the house. Unfortunately, many people dug to the necessary depth only to find that the excavation flooded easily owing to bad siting. As a result, many preferred to strengthen their houses, underneath the stairs being a favourite location.

**Coulsdon & Purley
Urban District Council**

**War Emergency
Committee 1939-1946**

**Councillors J M Morton
(Chairman), R H Sharp,
F G Kerswell**

*Courtesy of London
Borough of Croydon*

Propaganda material on a variety of subjects by way of posters was frequently displayed by the Ministry of Information. Slogans such as 'Careless talk costs lives', 'Be like Dad, Keep Mum' being a reminder that spies could be anywhere. The classic poster issued by the Ministry of Food exhorted anyone with a garden, allotment or even a window-box, to 'Dig for Victory'.

With young men and women being called up, the Government called for volunteers from the remaining civilian population to serve as air raid wardens, fire watchers, in the Auxiliary Fire Service, the Police War Reserve, other Civil Defence Units and Home Guard, with the teenage population being encouraged to join the various Cadet Units. In Coulsdon and Old Coulsdon, wardens' posts were set up, divided into three districts –

Page 73

A HISTORY OF COULSDON

District 6 H Q Coulsdon Library (Posts 21-29, 31-32)

District 7 H Q Junction of Marlpit Lane & Chaldon Way (Posts 30, 33, 35, 39-41)

District 8 H Q The Round House, Bradmore Green (Posts 34, 36-38)

WARDENS POSTS

DISTRICT 6

POST	ADDRESS	TELE
21	St Peter's School, The Chase	UPL.7109
22	St Anne's Playing Fields, The Wend	UPL.6651
23	60 Brighton Road, Coulsdon	UPL.6731
24	Junc. of Woodmansterne & St.Andrew's Rd.	UPL.6968
25	Near Woodmansterne Road Station, St Andrew's Road	UPL.6732
26	Playing Ground, Chipstead Valley Road	Down.1251
27	St Aidan's Church, Chipstead Valley Road	UPL.7051
HQ28	Coulsdon Library	UPL.6908
29	At rear of 15 Woodlands Grove	Down.1565
31	72 Star Lane, Hooley, or adj. rear of 13 Star Lane	Down.1169
32	'Gatcombe', London Road, Merstham	Down.243

DISTRICT 7

POST	ADDRESS	TELE
33	Junc. of Deane Lane & Netherne Lane	Down.1322
30	Adj. Telephone Exchange, Hollymeoak Rd.	Down.988
35	Junc. of Chaldon Way & Marden Way	Down.1239
39	Downs Road opposite Moorsom Way	Down.1218
HQ40	Junc. Marlpit Lane & Chaldon Way	Down.762
41	South end Byron Avenue	UPL.6733

DISTRICT 8

POST	ADDRESS	TELE
34	Opposite Tennyson Close, Coulsdon Rd.	Down.1307
36	Keston Avenue Schools	Down.1299
37	Farm Buildings, Taunton Lane	Down.1213
HQ38	Round House, Bradmore Green	Down.753

Exterior of Wardens' Reporting Post No. 35 in the vicinity of Chaldon Way, where it was called into action on 3 August 1944 (see pp.82-83)

A R P Wardens' Reporting Post No. 35

Interior of Wardens' Reporting Post No. 35

Coulsdon Civil Defence Corps 1945

HOME GUARD

On Tuesday 14 May 1940 the Secretary of State, Anthony Eden, appealed for Local Defence Volunteers and men between the ages of 17 and 65 willing to take up arms in their country's defence applied to the nearest police station. Thus, the 58th Surrey Battalion (Z Zone) was created and a sub-zone to include men in Coulsdon, Purley, Kenley and Whyteleafe was formed and called 'C' Company. In March 1941 'C' Company was split into 'C' and 'D' Companies, Coulsdon being 'C' Company, commanded by Major L Plowman. This did not solve all 'C' Company's geographical problems. The Company area was divided into two parts – the Highlands (Old Coulsdon and Farthing Downs), referred to as 'up top' by aboriginal inhabitants, and the comparative Lowlands of Brighton Road, Coulsdon. Nos. 11 and 12 Platoons constituted the Highlanders, Nos. 9 and 10 being located in the Lowlands, with headquarters in The Avenue and The Grove respectively. The LDV became the Home Guard in July 1940, and the Battalion received authority to wear the badge of The Queen's Royal Regiment (West Surrey).

In January 1943 Company Headquarters was moved from Brighton Road, Coulsdon, to the Marlpit Lane Drill Hall – a brand new building fitted with every modern convenience.

Only a few men were in possession of rifles and ammunition, but every night their defence posts were manned, for the danger then was very real and close to hand with the threat of invasion, and Coulsdon suffered more than its fair share of bombing. Later in the war the Company was on call to assist the Civil Defence at 'Flying Bomb Incidents' in the Company area, and turned out in strength to lend its aid in clearing away debris and carrying out first-aid repairs.

WORLD WAR II

The Company recruited few Women Auxiliaries, but one – Mrs L M Jenkins – typed and duplicated the Company Orders from the first in 1940 to the last on 4 December 1944. From first to last over 1,100 men were enrolled in the Company.

The Home Guard was ordered to 'Stand down' on 1 November 1944. The 'Stand down' parade was held at the Drill Hall, Marlpit Lane on Sunday 3 December 1944. Lt Col R L Haine VC MC, inspected his Battalion for the last time.

GIRLS' TRAINING CORPS

No. 353 Company (Coulsdon & Purley) which was started in May 1942 was one of the leading pre-service units in the area. It provided training to hundreds of girls aged 16-18 wishing to enter the Services, including the Land Army and Nursing Service, and taught basic training in drill, first-aid, PT, Morse, despatch-carrying and mechanics. The scope of the training was not confined to war needs but included preparations for home and civil life.

Girls' Training Corps

"A" Section General Efficiency Cup Winners

Presentation by Councillor F G Kerswell

Front row (left to right): ASL Parmenter, SL Plater, CSL Robson, SO Wenban, SL Humphreys, ASL King

Back row (left to right): Cadet Bryant, Cadet Barnes, Cadet Linton, Cadet Humphreys, Cadet ?, Cadet Pirie

The girls were a familiar sight in the district, with a uniform consisting of navy blue skirts, topped by white blouses with navy forage caps, and could often be seen marching back through Purley and Coulsdon to their headquarters at the Gas Company's former showrooms in Brighton Road (the building adjacent to Coulsdon Library). A great many girls went on to do well in the Services following the all-round training they had received. At the inception of the Corps a senior company only was formed, but in 1943 it was decided to form a junior company for girls between 14 and 16 years old.

Miss V Rhys-Davids was the Commandant of the Corps, with Mrs Wenban commanding 'A' Section (Coulsdon and Old Coulsdon).

The girls served in the Corps for most of the war, except for an enforced suspension of activities due to flying bombs. After nearly four years of service the Corps stood down in March 1945.

The early days of the war seemed something of an anti-climax, being called the 'phoney war', and the expected air-raids had not materialised. However, this was all to change by the summer of 1940 when the Battle of Britain raged overhead, followed by the Blitz when night after night people slept in shelters. Sadly, during 1940 high explosive bombs killed 10 people in Coulsdon, including three members of one family, two in another, and a police sergeant. Many more were injured.

At the height of the Battle of Britain at about 4.45 p.m. on Saturday 7 September 1940 a Hawker Hurricane crashed in the playing fields of the Purley County School for Boys after being shot down by a German aircraft. The pilot, Sqn Ldr Caesar Barrand Hull, 27, of Southern Rhodesia, was killed. Sqn Ldr Hull was an experienced pilot, having joined the RAF in 1935. He is buried in St Andrew's Church, near Tangmere Airfield, Sussex.

As the autumn weather closed in, the daylight raids tailed off but the night raids continued with savage attacks on London, and Coulsdon, lying under the route of the night raiders, often received attention from the aircraft passing overhead. In November 1940 the operations room of RAF Kenley, temporarily housed in a shop in Godstone Road, Caterham, was closed and removed to the more permanent premises of The Grange close to St John's Church, where the interior was converted into a spacious control room. With a high ceiling, it was fitted out in the usual style with a raised gallery from which controllers could look down onto a large table holding a map of southern England and France. It was on this that the WAAF plotters continuously marked the position of the aircraft.

The Grange

behind St John's Church, used as an Operations Room for RAF Kenley from November 1940 until after the war

Photographed in 2000

Whether or not German intelligence knew of this move is uncertain, but on Sunday 1 December a stick of bombs rained down on Old Coulsdon. Explosions rocked St John's and the congregation including a large party of Guardsmen from Caterham Barracks threw themselves under the pews. Buildings near the church were demolished or damaged, and at The Grange the blast caused ceilings, doors and windows to collapse. It was a miracle that no-one was seriously injured.

In April 1942 in addition to a visit by Winston Churchill, King George VI – after visiting Kenley – was taken to The Grange, where he watched the progress of the entire Wing on the plotting board.

In 1942 the Government asked local authorities to provide events to persuade people to spend holidays at home, to reduce demand for hard-pressed railway and other transport services. Dances and other entertainments were arranged at Grange Park and in the Memorial Recreation Ground.

Once the Battle of Britain and the Blitz were over, there were only comparatively minor raids. However, bombs continued to fall intermittently on the district, and in February 1944 one of the heaviest raids in this area took place, resulting in three members of one family in Vincent Road being killed.

In an extract from *Mayday....Calling Mayday* by Joyce Millard, now Mrs Joyce Smith, a former WAAF, she recalls—

> 'The Ops Room compound was spread over an area of Old Coulsdon – the nearby Golf Club House had been requisitioned and that was our mess. There was a NAAFI within the golf course grounds and our billets were requisitioned private houses in an unmade-up road alongside and overlooking the golf course. The Orderly room was in Coulsdon Court Road.
>
> We were within easy walking distance of the Ops Room and I was told that previously all Ops Room personnel on a shift used to assemble for duty and march in a squad along the streets to The Grange, until one day the squad was strafed by a marauding Luftwaffe fighter and thereafter staff were instructed to make their own way on duty'.

Two members of the Bourne Society, Mrs M A Bray and Colin Kenyon, both of Old Coulsdon, were stationed at Kenley and served in the Operations Room at The Grange.

MEMORIES OF THE BATTLE OF BRITAIN AND THE WAR YEARS – Rosie Watts – Born 1917

I remember the events of 15 August 1940 clearly. Just before 6.00 p.m. I was standing outside 45 Woodman Road looking for my mother, who had gone shopping. It was a lovely day with a clear blue sky. I heard a faint droning and, looking up, I saw a formation of bombers very high in the sky. For a moment I thought how lovely they looked and then I realised they were flying north instead of south and were beginning to lose altitude fast and going towards Croydon aerodrome. As they disappeared from my sight I saw little black objects falling from the planes and I knew it was a raid.

Frank (my husband) was driving past the aerodrome just as the raid started and the first he knew was a warden stopping his car and telling him to get in the public shelter which was opposite the aerodrome. Instead Frank dived under his car because he could hear machine gunning, and then the bombs started dropping. As he dived under the car he remembered hearing 'Workers' Playtime' coming from the factories. When the bombing was over he came out from under his car to find that the shelter he should have gone in had received a direct hit, as had the factories on the aerodrome. He went to help the people in them and said he would never forget the terrible sights he saw. He stayed there doing what he could to get people out until the rescue service had everything under control.

I have many memories of the war years, some of them humorous, some frightening and some very sad. There is one from the Battle of Britain which still brings tears to my eyes. My mother, my baby daughter and I had been sheltering in our Anderson shelter because a terrible air battle was in progress overhead. After a while I came out and looked over the valley to the chalk pits in Marlpit Lane; there were planes diving and chasing each other all over the sky and then I saw a parachute coming down. I saw a man hanging there, then I saw flames coming from the harness and creeping up the ropes he was hanging from. I started to pray for him – I did not know if he was British or German – it did not matter, I just wanted him to land safely. But he did not because eventually the parachute burst into flames and I saw his body hurtle to the ground. I have thought about him often over the years.

During the war I went back to live with my mother. After my daughter Gwen was born I decided to breed rabbits to supplement the meat ration. If I supplied rabbits to the local butcher I was allowed to buy food and hay for their keep. I had to join the Rabbit Club which issued vouchers which I took to Mr Grover the corn chandler. Every day I would take Gwen and my Chow dog Ming for a walk around the woods and fields up by the Mount and I always had a sack with me to collect dandelion leaves, cow parsley and clover for the rabbits.

My friend and I used to walk up to the Rec with our babies. We felt safe because an air raid shelter had been built just inside the gate. It was a different atmosphere then, although the café was there it was mostly used by war workers from Hall's Yard and several soldiers could be seen. The Royal West Kent Regiment was stationed in houses along Reddown and Fairdene Roads. We got talking to some of them who said they were not allowed to leave the area but if their wives came to stay in the village they could get an all-night pass. So I told two of them to go and see my mother as we had a spare room. Between them they spent several nights with us.

A FEW MEMORIES OF THE WAR YEARS IN OLD COULSDON – Stan Coleman – Born 1937

During the war I lived at 115 Bradmore Way, next door to where the library is today. There were no buildings there in those days – it was just a plot of grass and shrubs. I can clearly remember an anti-aircraft gun positioned there. I understand that one night some Canadian soldiers returned after an evening off – possibly drinking a little too much – and took command of the anti-aircraft gun and had a few pops but no harm was done!

Where the Coulsdon C of E school playground is now there were Army lorries parked in the woods and there was a big tin shed on what is now the Scout Hut site behind the church hall. That tin shed was the fire station.

My father fought and was taken prisoner in World War I and was too old to serve in World War II, but was however an Air Raid Precautions officer. I remember large tanks of water stored in the pathway behind our back gate which were there in readiness to be used with the stirrup pumps if there was a fire. I remember falling into the water on one occasion (typical young boy) and getting a good hiding! There was also a large reservoir of water stored in the garden of *The Tudor Rose*. There was an anti-aircraft tower built at tree-top level on the common on the opposite side of the road to Windmill Farm. I can remember one being in Burntwood Lane, Caterham, on land opposite where De Stafford School stands today. If you drive down and look carefully to your right you can see it.

Like many houses we had a shelter in the garden and I can remember spending time down there. It was two-thirds under the ground, and in winter my father put wooden slats on the floor to try to prevent us getting our feet too wet.

There were Italian soldiers as POWs in the Territorial Barracks, and it was not an uncommon sight to see them walking the streets in groups under the eye of one or two guards. They were very cheerful chaps and made little wooden toys for the local children.

(Above): Coulsdon & Purley ARP Heavy Rescue Squad *c.*1940
(Below): Air-raid damage in Vincent Road, Coulsdon 1944
Photographs courtesy of Purley Library

At the top of Marlpit Lane between the garage and pond there were stables with plenty of land, and a very large building was erected there, becoming a parachute packing station. After the war the riding stables used it as an indoor riding school. Now there are houses on the site. A bomb landed on the brow of the hill at the top of Bradmore Way and failed to explode; I can vaguely remember that we were unable to stay in our homes.

Towards the end of the war someone told me that there was ice cream for sale at the parade of shops. Having never eaten or even seen ice cream I was eager to try this luxury, so off I went, clutching my coppers in my hand. I purchased the ice cream which was – I guess – about two inches in diameter and about 1½ inches deep with a band of cardboard round it. I ran home and as there was no one in I placed my precious ice cream on a plate to wait the arrival of mum and dad, and then went out to play. I cannot describe how disappointed I was to find just a pool of white liquid when I returned indoors. (A mistake I never repeated).

I can remember that after the war there was a huge bonfire situated on the triangle of Bradmore Green, the bonfire being adorned with effigies of Hitler. Many of the locals gathered around to celebrate.

WARTIME ANECDOTE – Bill Gilbert

I can remember as a schoolboy walking over Farthing Downs with my father, I think it was in the spring of 1941, and seeing soldiers manning an anti-aircraft gun. My father got into conversation with them and we found that they were Canadians who said they had recently arrived in England. They asked what it was that lay to the north, as every night they could see searchlights and gunfire in the distance. When my father told them that it was London and the nightly bombing they were amazed. They had no idea what part of the country they were in. In those days there was only a rough track over the downs.

1944-45

Towards the end of the war the first pilotless planes were launched in June 1944 (barely a week after D-Day), and for the following three months, the sinister sound of these V1 flying bombs (Buzz-bombs or Doodlebugs as they were nicknamed), became an all too-familiar feature of life in London and the south-east (some 54 falling in Coulsdon and Purley). It was an unnerving experience to hear the drone of the engine suddenly cut out, followed several seconds later by an explosion. In the closing months of the war, Hitler launched his V2 rockets, which were far superior technically, and were silent on approach, so that the rocket fell without warning. Unfortunately, three members of one family in Coulsdon were killed by a flying bomb blast, and we are indebted to Mr D Adams for providing the following abridged Wardens Report on this incident in Chaldon Way—

'On the morning of Thursday 3 August 1944 at about 5.20 a.m. the chugging sound of a V1 engine cut out over Farthing Downs and the bomb glided down, exploding on impact in the back garden of 180 Chaldon Way. ARP Post 35 covered this area and Deputy Post Warden C C (Bill) Adams set up an incident room to organise rescue and repair, having rapidly discovered there were casualties in the Anderson shelters in the gardens of 178 and 180. Light Rescue Ambulance and National Fire Service vehicles were called and arrived 25 minutes after the bomb exploded, and a sergeant and a constable from the police arrived to help.

By 5.50 an ambulance was on site, along with a doctor (Dr Beeston) and it and another ambulance had stretcher cases in Purley Hospital 20 minutes later. At 6.50 another ambulance took away one body from the Anderson shelter behind 180 but others in the same shelter were luckier and were added to the patients in Purley. However two were trapped and later confirmed fatally injured.

The WVS First Aid Post at 127 (Mrs Slater's house with help from Mrs Page), took in further casualties with cuts from glass, bruising and shock, where they were attended to by Dr Beeston. With

2000 lbs of high-explosive, it was not just a couple of homes that were damaged. In this case 150 houses suffered to a greater or lesser degree, and all had to be made habitable as soon as possible so reserves were called in. Some 60 men of the Home Guard helped to clear rubble and glass, remove furniture and start repairs to blackout. Laths and nails were needed to effect the repairs and they arrived within three hours of the explosion. A mobile canteen arrived to feed and give tea to the many more than the WVS could cope with. The services of the Gas, Electricity and Water Companies were needed to repair the damage and all came promptly and operated effectively. The small ARP Post needed assistance and more than 100 turned up to direct and assist in repairs and fill in the vital War Damage Reports – 93 were completed with more to follow.

Everyone did their work well, some leaving to catch the train to Town for their 'day job', after hours of rescue work, others staying behind to complete their volunteered services'.

Germany surrendered on 8 May 1945 to spontaneous rejoicing, the church bells ringing for the first time in five years. The Japanese Government surrendered a few months' later on 14 August. However, rationing of food and clothing continued for some time afterwards. Indeed bread was rationed between July 1946 and July 1948, a commodity which had not been rationed even during the war.

Sources:

Coulsdon & Purley Advertiser

Coulsdon and Purley Libraries

Croydon Local Studies Library

DODKINS, W. C. *History of the 58th Surrey Home Guard*

MILLARD, Joyce. *Mayday....calling Mayday*

OGLEY, Bob. *Surrey at War*

PILKINGTON, L. *Surrey Airfields in the Second World War*

Daphne Plater

Local Residents

**The chalk quarry at
Coulsdon viewed
from Farthing Downs**

1923

**From a watercolour
by Ethel Hall**

**The same view as
above in the 1950s –
showing
development**

*Courtesy of Purley
Library*

**The same view in
2000 – cattle have
returned to grazing in
pursuance of The
Corporation of
London's active
management of
Farthing Downs**

Chapter 12

From 1945 to the Millennium

by Ian Scales

Coulsdon joined in the celebrations marking the end of World War II along with the rest of the country, giving thanks for having been saved from the mass slaughter of the previous war. The change between the farming village of 1918 and the suburb of 1945 was reflected in the make-up of the population, which was not only vastly more numerous but which also included 'incomers' with little or no family history associating them with the area. Perhaps that is one reason why there has been no separate war memorial erected to the fallen, other than to add the years '1939 – 1945' to the existing memorials. Also, apart from the change in attitude to remembrance of the dead that had occurred, many of the casualties in the second war were civilians killed on their home ground, and as such each had his or her own memorial in nearby cemeteries. Still, it is a pity that a more formal record of those who died defending their country was not made.

Post-war shortages of building materials meant that bomb damage was evident for much of the decade following the war. The rubble had been cleared but the gaps remained, and can be spotted to this day by the presence of newer houses or shops interrupting the run of 1920s or 1930s buildings, but even these have mellowed, marked only by a slight change in design, often most visible at roof level.

New housing to replace that lost in the bombing was a priority, not just for Coulsdon residents but also for families moving out of Inner London and Croydon. The Green Belt laws still stopped developments planned in the 1930s, such as the extensions to Chaldon Way, Caterham Drive, The Mount and others, but some greenfield sites were given up.

During the housing boom of the 1960s, Waddington Avenue was extended to Caterham Drive and its accompanying offshoots Shirley Avenue and Carew Close were built on farmland; the south end of Tollers Lane by Lacey Green became a whole new community when a major council estate was developed between Tollers Lane and the brow overlooking Happy Valley. Backing onto Parson's Pightle, where the old parsonage was demolished at that time, the new estate boasts roads named for the parsonage's most famous occupant, Admiral William Goodenough. At the time of building F H B Ellis had come to the end of half a century's service as local councillor and he too is remembered with two roads named after him.

Coulsdon, Shopping Centre

Brighton Road 1949

This post-war view taken opposite *The Red Lion* shows the increase in traffic at the busy Chipstead Valley Road. (*cf.* page 6)

Note the police box on the right

A HISTORY OF COULSDON

Another large housing development in Coulsdon since the war was the Wates' Estate, built in what had been a pleasantly wooded area between Byron Avenue and the railway. There was a fearful row before they were allowed to build, but it must be admitted that Wates took great trouble to retain many of the trees and Coulsdon Woods is now accepted as a very pleasant addition to our community. Whilst it was being built a whole new chapter of prehistory was added when the digging of a drainage ditch in 1969 uncovered a cemetery dating back to Roman times. It had been known since 1805, when the Stoats Nest quarry was being developed, that there were traces of early settlement on that hill, but that these ditches were defensive, round an Iron Age settlement, did not become apparent until this latest dig. A more detailed description of these finds is recorded in Volume 9 of the Bourne Society's *Local History Records* (1970).

Infilling to give additional houses in established roads has been a feature of recent development, with dozens of additional 'Closes' to be found, where one house has been demolished and several others built in its place clustered round their own service road. This system must account for hundreds of extra families being able to enjoy the clean air and superb countryside of our suburb.

The Wates' Estate was not the only remnant of countryside left over from the developments of the past 50 years. Some still survive but others exist only in the memories of residents. Take the modern library in Old Coulsdon, built in 1963 on a small plot between Bradmore Green School and the houses at the top of Bradmore Way. There are grown-ups now who recall a small wood there which was a wonderful place in which to play. It seemed enormous, with pathways twisting between tall trees and thick bushes, a wood of truly Enid Blytonian proportions – just one example of many that have gone. Fortunately there are still acres of wooded land within the boundaries, one of the largest of which is that below Coulsdon Court Golf Course and Canon's Hill, down to Old Lodge Lane. The least altered woodlands left today are those bordering Ditches Lane – Devilsden, Sparkie and Figgs Woods. Some say the line of yew trees along the north-east flank of Farthing Downs goes back to Celtic times, 2000 years ago, but in truth it is nowhere near this grand age.

The rush for new housing in the 1960s had a down-side too, with the demolition of a number of historic buildings, mainly on the excuse that the site was needed. In some cases buildings had been derelict, but in others the clearance was quite unnecessary and an earlier example of this was the demolition of the Round Lodge on Grange Park facing Bradmore Green. Dating from Victorian times, the Lodge protected an entrance to The Grange and had been lived in by the first old age pensioner in the district to receive Lloyd George's weekly bounty – 5s.0d (25p) at the time. The site has only recently been developed following use as a council depot. Parson's Pightle has been referred to above; it is but another house, this time from the 18th century, to be pulled down. Hooley House had perhaps outlived its value as an historic monument, having been extensively developed throughout its 800 year life. Nonetheless the demolition in 1971 of what was by then known as the Ashdown Park Hotel appeared to be pure vandalism, though at least in this case a new estate was eventually built, after more than a decade of indecision. The lodge house at Hooley House remains and will celebrate its bicentenary in 2020.

To a visitor returning to Coulsdon after an absence of a number of years, the change that would strike home most forcibly is the increase in traffic. In the late 1940s the war may have been over, but Pool petrol was still rationed, and anyway it was nearly impossible to buy a car since practically all production was exported to earn foreign currency, necessary if Britain was to pay off its debts and avoid bankruptcy. Only the war survivors were taken for short journeys on the empty roads.

Of course these shortages were temporary and by the 1950s the traffic was building up. Plans were laid to bypass the A23 through Coulsdon with a new 'Motorway', the M23, but this was not to be. In 1965 Coulsdon became part of the London Borough of Croydon and when in 1971 the Greater London Council, with its changed political majority, had a look at the budgets for both roads and housing, it determined that no new motorway would enter its territory, with the inevitable clearing of whole streets of houses all the way through to Streatham.

FROM 1945 TO THE MILLENNIUM

The industrial complex built on the former Marlpit Lane quarry.

Photographed from Rutherwick Rise in 1999

Photograph courtesy of Roger King

Coulsdon Manor Hotel, formerly Coulsdon Court, photographed in 2000

The wall in the foreground is a ha-ha, forming a stock-proof boundary to the garden without obstructing the view

This thatched round house was built as a lodge to *The Grange* next to St John's Church. It was sited on the edge of Grange Park opposite Bradmore Green but was demolished soon after World War II

Photograph courtesy of Croydon Local Studies Library

A typical group of local schoolchildren returning to their homes in Stoats Nest Village

*c.*1954

Possibly assisted by the few car owners

Photograph courtesy of Croydon Local Studies Library

The M23 was stopped at Hooley and the planned route through a cutting at the top of Portnalls Road and a viaduct over Chipstead Valley Road towards the Clock House, never came to fruition.

When it became clear that Coulsdon would have to make do with the A23, a local pressure group was formed to press for a bypass of the main shopping centre. Croydon Council supported the scheme and over the next 20 years various plans were submitted to the Highways Agency, finally securing agreement to proceed in 1999 with an expected start date in 2001 or 2002. However, from July 2000 Coulsdon will be under the aegis of the new London Mayor's department 'Transport for London', so there may yet be another delay. Meanwhile much money was spent during the 1990s upgrading the A23 to a 'Red Route', with additional traffic lights and limited car parking.

Rail transport has also changed in the past 50 years, the main loss being the closure of Coulsdon North station in 1984, the burden of a considerably increased passenger flow now being taken by improved services from Coulsdon South and Smitham stations. This closure opened a valuable space for small factories and warehouses where the Coulsdon North locomotive sheds and train marshalling yard once stood. These industrial buildings in their turn will have to give way to the bypass, officially known as the Coulsdon Relief Road, when that is built.

There are few villages that can trace their direct ancestry – and even their name – over 13 centuries, and Coulsdon is proud to be amongst that elite band. In 1975 Old Coulsdon was the scene of many commemorative activities, centred around St John's church and Farthing Downs. Several historical plays were put on by the children of local schools, and the church held a weekend of exhibitions showing its development over the centuries. A number of trees were planted to mark the occasion, joining the great horse chestnut outside Bradmore Green school planted in 1897 to mark Queen Victoria's diamond jubilee. Subject to an annual thrashing by youngsters dislodging its rich harvest of conkers, the tree celebrated its hundred years in 1997 still growing in stature and in good health.

A major change to Coulsdon occurred in 1992 when after more than 100 years Cane Hill Hospital closed. Largely responsible for the development of Coulsdon during its life, modern methods in the treatment of mental illness ensured that it had outlived its usefulness. Many of the buildings remain, empty shells now, the water tower only having been given a useful life as the support for television and mobile telephone aerials. A small mental unit survives in modern buildings near the original site for patients unable to be allowed to live in the community. Plans are being drawn up for a technology park to replace the hospital, together with a larger mental unit on the site of the old Portnalls Farm house.

Farthing Downs has changed in the past half-century. The arrival of myxomatosis in the 1960s killed off most of the rabbit population that had kept the land clear of thorn bushes, which thereafter threatened to take over the grassland; indeed the fields between Chaldon Way and Tollers Lane have been given over to bushes and ash trees since the rabbits left. The Corporation of London, which owns the Downs, has taken steps to replace the rabbits with cattle which now roam the area, keeping the grass healthy and the bushes to a decent size. The Welcome Tea Rooms at the south end have gone, along with the swing-boats that delighted children for half a century, but summer days still see a multitude of cars parked there while their owners take in the wonderful air and beautiful views. Both Happy Valley and Farthing Downs are Sites of Special Scientific Interest (SSSIs) so the chalkland plants that grow there are protected as never before.

The approaching Millennium – the third to be witnessed by our downland village – will see many more changes as history unfolds. The cairn to be erected at the highest point on Farthing Downs marks the end of the second Millennium, complete with a 'time capsule' sampling the way of life now. What will our successors make of that?

**The Tudor Parade retains a local identity in 2000 with the busy
Old Coulsdon Village Stores on the corner to the left**

Coulsdon Church, Near Croydon.

A rural scene of St John's Church, Old Coulsdon, dating from around the beginning of the 20th century, before the surrounding area was developed

Chapter 13

Churches and Chapels

by Ken Righton and Ian Scales

St John's Parish Church, Canon's Hill

There has been a church on the present site for 1000 years, and probably longer. The manor of Coulsdon was put in the care of the Abbey of St Peter and St Paul, Chertsey in AD 675, and there is no reason to believe that it treated Coulsdon differently to any other manor, so one of its first tasks would have been to build a church.

Traces of earlier churches than the present one have been found during excavations. There may have been a wooden building at first, and Anglo-Saxon worked stones older than the present church have been found, probably from the church mentioned in Domesday Book. The present 'old' church chancel was built around 1250, but the nave and base of the tower that we use now date from the 15th century, built over the much earlier building, traces of which are in the corners of the nave.

**The Ringers
1930**

**G Jeffrey, M Yeoman,
W Martingell,
A Beadle, M Martingell**

*Courtesy of Purley
Library*

The sedilia (seats for the clergy) and piscina (the 'washing-up' bowl for the chalice and paten) that are built into the south wall of the chancel are 13th century, as is the main arch separating the chancel and nave. The east window and the apostles' windows and others are in their original places, but some of the stonework looks much more modern, probably replaced early in the 19th century when there was much work done to the church. The chancel's Victorian stained glass was destroyed by enemy action during World War II.

There used to be a south aisle on the old church, but that was demolished in 1958 when the new church was built. It contained the organ, a vestry built in the original south porch, and the tomb of the founder of the church. You can still see the arch that spanned the founder's tomb, built into the east wall of the new church and containing the 'In Memoriam' list of those killed in World War I, but this is in a new site.

The tower was first added early in the 15th century and has undergone many changes over the years, the latest of which was the addition of the porch during the 1970s, when stone from the old Bradmore Green school was used. As originally built the tower lacked a west entrance, since the south door was used by lay people.

The present ring of six bells dates from 1675, making it the oldest in the county. Earlier there were three 'belles in the stepull', recorded in the inventory taken in 1549. This 'stepull' may well have been the church tower, the two words being interchangeable at the time. Later there was a very slim steeple, built above the battlemented form of the top of the tower.

Additional church space was badly needed following the development of the hill farms in the 1920s, but the depression in the 1930s and then World War II delayed construction until the late 1950s. There was serious discussion about building a second church elsewhere in the parish, possibly in Lacey Green, so that people would not have too far to go, but in the end it was decided to add the 'new' church to the south side of St John's.

Much more of St John's story can be found in the brief history booklet, available in the church.

St Mary Help of Christians Roman Catholic Church, Coulsdon Road

The site where the church now stands in Coulsdon Road was once a brickfield that extended as far as The Crossways. In 1850 the field supplied the bricks to build Coulsdon Court for Squire Byron.

On Sunday 21 September 1941, a new Mass centre was opened in Old Coulsdon and blessed by Archbishop Amigo. Money was raised by an outdoor collection, by dances at Keston Avenue School and whist drives which were held in Mrs Oliver's room – The Corner Shop Café by *The Tudor Rose*.

Mass was first said in Keston Avenue School and the Salesian nuns (founded by Don Bosco) were brought by taxi each Sunday at a cost of 6s.0d return to instruct the children . This centre at Keston School was in the days of Fr Tyndall in the 1940s. After a time the school raised the rent and the parish was unable to pay, so Egbert Cedric Jones offered a room in his house at The Grange. Fr Tyndall was succeeded by Fr O Leeke, and Fr Leeke by Dr Cyril Hastings.

**St Mary Help of
Christians Roman
Catholic Church**

Coulsdon Road

1999

Negotiations for the purchase of the present site went on from 1948 to 1950 in the time of Fr Leeke. Application was made for a building licence and the hall was built by Plater & Sons with Philip P Browning, civil engineer. It cost £5,708 19s.1d. Partially to offset this cost, the ground at the back of the present church and hall which abuts Thornton Crescent was sold in 1957 for £2,250.

In 1960 Bishop Cowderey decided to separate Old Coulsdon from Coulsdon RC parish and Fr Bovingdon was sent to take over. Without any proper headquarters from which to operate, a priest's house was added. Next, the Church was built after plans had been submitted to Bishop's House, the contract being signed on 15 November 1964.

In the meantime, negotiations were going on with the authorities of Netherne Hospital for a Chapel for the Catholic patients and staff. At the time they were using the Church of England Church, which was rather difficult as there was no confessional and other hospital patients came in to attend Holy Communion. This often produced scuffles and other unseemly behaviour. Eventually the new Netherne Chapel was built and furnished in 1964. The church in Old Coulsdon was built in 1965, and the opening and blessing with confirmation was performed by Archbishop Cyril Cowderey on 17 April 1966.

Fr Bovingdon made copious notes about the history of the church and this information can be seen on application to the parish priest.

St Andrew's Church of England, Woodmansterne Road

With the development at Smitham Bottom, by the start of the 20th century there was an increasing need for an Anglican church closer to this new community. Initially the need was met by meetings and services being held in the new Smitham School buildings in Chipstead Valley Road. They were overseen by the rector of St John's.

This could only be a temporary arrangement so in 1906 the parish of St Andrew was constituted, consisting of the area of Coulsdon parish that lay west of Brighton Road, plus a small part of Woodmansterne and a larger part of Beddington parish. A mission hall of corrugated iron was built, which was used for services until a better hall was built in 1908 behind the Old Comrades Club nearby – later the HQ of the South London Harriers. The new hall was so much more comfortable the congregation moved there for services in 1909, leaving the mission hall for meetings. The local territorials were allowed the use of the hall from 1915 for the rest of World War I, heat and rent free.

ST. ANDREW'S CHURCH, COULSDON.

St Andrew's Church, Coulsdon

1920s

In 1908 the site of the present church was purchased, and in 1913 plans for the building of the chancel and nave of the permanent church at an estimated cost of £7,000 were accepted. The building was commenced with the foundation stone being laid in April 1914 and the church was consecrated by the Bishop of Kingston in October of that year.

The start of World War I was a bad time to build, and when that war was followed by two depressions and World War II, the church – though usable – remained incomplete until 1964 when the west end was completed with the addition of a narthex. Despite its massive looks, the tower is not strong enough to allow installation of bells; instead, the illuminated cross that shines out over the valley marks the presence of the church very effectively.

There has been considerable development of the site since 1964, with the addition of new halls and meeting rooms. One building on the site that has been demolished was a small meeting hall dedicated to the needs of a portion of the population that has also died out – servants. The new houses being built during the 1920s contained a large number of live-in girls who had nowhere to spend their occasional evenings off other than *The Red Lion* and local tea shops. The small hall – the 'Club Room' – built in 1936, offered a warm and reasonably comfortable meeting place for them, free from the temptations of strong liquor and strange men.

St Francis of Assisi Church of England, Rickman Hill

The need for a further church followed the development and building of houses along and surrounding the western end of Chipstead Valley Road in the early 1920s – with few car-owners at that time, St Andrew's was considered too far away. In 1928 the church was built as a 'daughter' church of St Andrew's, money being made available by the Bishop of Kingston's 'Twenty-five Churches Fund'. St Francis's was the only church in this area to benefit from this fund. It was opened on 15 October that year.

Former St Francis of Assisi Church, Rickman Hill, now St Mary & St Shenouda Coptic Orthodox Church

1999

For something like 30 years it served the local community as both church and social centre. With curtains over the altar, children's clinics were held and devoted voluntary enthusiasm from parishioners ensured that the building was adequately maintained and well used.

In 1960 a church hall was added. The Church Commissioners ruled that if £2,000 could be raised voluntarily, they would meet the rest of the cost. This, with difficulty, was achieved and following the hall's building it was consecrated. The 'Rickman Hill Club' is remembered as the first to start a luncheon club and to provide social outings for its older members.

However in 1988, with a falling congregation it was decided that the church must be closed, and the buildings were sold to the Coptic Orthodox Church, which dedicated it to St Mary and St Shenouda.

CHURCHES AND CHAPELS

St Aidan's Roman Catholic Church, Chipstead Valley Road

Started in the early years of the 20th century when it was in the RC parish of Beddington, on Woodcote Grove Road, St Aidan's was located in a hall next to North Downs Timber Company which was later used as the Co-op Hall and is currently a martial arts centre. The hall was built using dressed stones from a demolished barn at Stoats Nest Farm.

The former St Aidan's Roman Catholic Church in Woodcote Grove Road

Photograph 1971 by Peter Flint

Courtesy of Purley Library

The presbytery was a bungalow in Woodman Road behind the church, marked by a cross over the hall window. Most recently used as offices of the timber company next door, it was burned down in the early 1980s.

In 1930 Adrian Scott was commissioned to build a church on the present site between Portnalls Road and Chipstead Valley Road. The Lady Chapel, the sanctuary and the nave were completed in 1931, but the sacristies were not added until 1953.

In 1964 it was discovered that the foundations were defective, having been built on gravel and sand washed down by the ancient river that carved the Chipstead Valley. This necessitated a complete rebuilding on the same site, this time with foundations taken down to solid chalk. So the current church was built there in 1966, effectively on a concrete raft. Since then, in 1998, a splendid hall has been added.

Methodist Church, Brighton Road

The decision to build a church in Coulsdon was taken in 1909 after two years of meetings in the home of Thomas E Bond, followed by the Working Men's Club in Lion Green Road – where meetings had been held surrounded by two billiard-tables, cases of stuffed birds and trophies of war-like weapons. The Working Men's Club was only available on Sundays, allowing no functions such as social or educational meetings during the week. This unsatisfactory arrangement could only be temporary, so the site of the present Gothic-style church on Brighton Road was purchased in 1910 for £800. The first contribution, 1s.0d, was received from an anonymous passenger on the 8.35 a.m. train to London. Much of the money needed for building the church was donated by Sir Horace Brooks Marshall (later Lord Marshall of Chipstead).

The building committee was selected from a church society that had only 19 members, but despite its small numbers, the present church was planned and built in 1911 with flint and stone outer walls and a red brick interior. The foundation stone was laid on 5 April 1911 (in the midst of a late snowstorm) and the doors opened for a dedication service on 1 November of the same year. It holds 440 people and cost £7,835. With the extensive house-building going on at the time, the original 19 members had grown to nearly 100 by 1915 and then more than doubled again over the following 15 years. The church added a school and a meeting hall in 1914, which was enlarged in 1934.

The manse in The Drive was purchased in 1925 and a tennis club laid out on land donated in 1928.

Methodist Church, Whitethorn Avenue

With the planned development of the Clock House Estate after World War II, the free churches in the district agreed that Woodmansterne was to be a Methodist responsibility. There was initial opposition from the Carshalton UDC to a church being there, so services were held in members' homes at that time. The building of a meeting hall in Whitethorn Avenue was commenced in 1952, followed by the opening service in 1953. At its start the Sunday School there had a membership of over 300 children, though in recent years this has declined. The hall, also used for some church services, was sold to a tenant housing association in 1999 for redevelopment.

Meanwhile a modern church alongside the old hall was financed and built following the release of war-damage money in 1959 and completed in 1962, since when it has been extensively refurbished. A fully equipped hall occupies the ground floor, with the church upstairs seating over 100.

The manse in Southwood Avenue was purchased in 1955 and sold in 1971.

Old Coulsdon Congregational Church, Coulsdon Road

After World War II when the free churches agreed that the Methodist Purley Circuit would be responsible for the spiritual comfort of people in the Clock House Estate, the Congregationalists would look after their flock in Old Coulsdon.

In October 1948 publicity leaflets were posted in the village advertising a new Sunday School, to be held at Purley Grammar School for Boys. An inaugural meeting was held on 7 November for the 82 enrolled members. The success of the Sunday School led to parents deciding to hold a Sunday service, the first of which, in December 1951, was held in an outside classroom in Downland School, run by Miss Martin in Pound Cottage in Coulsdon Road. A year later the services moved to the Day Nursery in a prefab adjacent to Grange Park.

In 1953 the Church was formally realised by a Covenant at Purley Congregational Church, when there were 27 founding members, with Revd Ronald Newman as full-time minister, but as yet it had no proper church premises. Church meetings moved to the café above Oliver's shop, while in 1955 services were held in St John's Hall. That same year the Congregational Union was presented by James Stanley with a plot of land at the corner of Canon's Hill and Coulsdon Road. This was where 'Elmcroft', 103 Coulsdon Road – a bungalow which was destroyed by a German bomb on 1 December 1940 – once stood.

The present church was duly built there, with the opening and dedication service on 4 October 1958. Since then there have been a number of building extensions, the largest being the Cameron Hall, named for Camery and Ron Newman, Minister there from 1953 to 1983. The halls were extensively damaged by an arson attack in May 2000.

(Right): Coulsdon Methodist Church, Brighton Road, 1999

(Above): Revd Harold Colbeck, the first Minister of Whitethorn Methodist Church, 1952-55

Old Coulsdon Congregational Church, Coulsdon Road, soon after its dedication in 1958

Photograph courtesy of M C Davison

(Above): The opening of the Elim Pentecostal Church, Chipstead Valley Road, in 1926

(Right): The original Coulsdon Baptist Church (1936), now a Church Hall

Photographed in 1999

Kingdom Hall of Jehovah's Witnesses in Woodman Road, Coulsdon

Photographed in 1999

Coulsdon Christian Fellowship, Chipstead Valley Road

The Coulsdon Christian Fellowship grew out of the amalgamation of two pentecostal churches. They originally met in the early 1920s over a shop in Brighton Road, but doctrinal differences resulted in a split, when each bought land for its church within 200 yards of each other in Chipstead Valley Road.

The Elim Pentecostal Church had its beginnings in Ireland in 1915, then in Essex in 1921, and had spread to Coulsdon by 1925. Since 1929 its full title is the Elim Foursquare Gospel Alliance.

The church site in Chipstead Valley Road was where the Croydon, Merstham & Godstone Iron Railway crossed the road on an embankment and bridge nearly 200 years ago. In 1925, the site having been bought, the church itself was built by its members using their skills as builders and decorators and it was completed in 1926. The four Italian marble pillars on its frontage represent Christ the Saviour, the Healer, the Baptizer and the Coming King, the four corners of the Foursquare Gospel Church.

The Coulsdon Baptist Church has in fact moved from its original iron hall built in 1936, to Pine Walk where it is known as the Woodmansterne Baptist Church. The iron hall in Chipstead Valley Road served members who did not want to move, and has been used variously under the names of Fellowship of Independent Evangelical Churches (FIEC), then as Coulsdon Evangelical Free Church until 1970, and until the early 1980s as Coulsdon Baptist.

In 1984 the two churches once again joined together under the name of Elim Valley Fellowship, part of the Coulsdon Christian Fellowship. The iron building was renovated and is now the Church hall.

Jehovah's Witnesses, Woodman Road

Following the pattern of other religious movements in Coulsdon, the Witnesses' early meetings were held at various sites before moving to their present Kingdom Hall in Woodman Road. Building was commenced in 1968 and the Hall was opened in 1969.

SOURCES

BIDEN, N, GADSBY, J M & SCALES, I (Ed) (1998) *A brief guide to the parish church of St John the Evangelist, Coulsdon.*

Bourne Society Bulletins and *Local History Records*

Croydon Library Services

Former members of St. Francis' Church

Fr Bovingdon, St Mary Help of Christians

Joy Gadsby

MALDEN, H E (Ed) (1902-1912). *Victoria County History of the County of Surrey*

Members of Old Coulsdon Congregational Church

Revd John Bown, Coulsdon Methodist Church

Scott Freeman, Coulsdon Christian Fellowship

SWIFT, Rowland C *Methodism in the Purley Circuit*

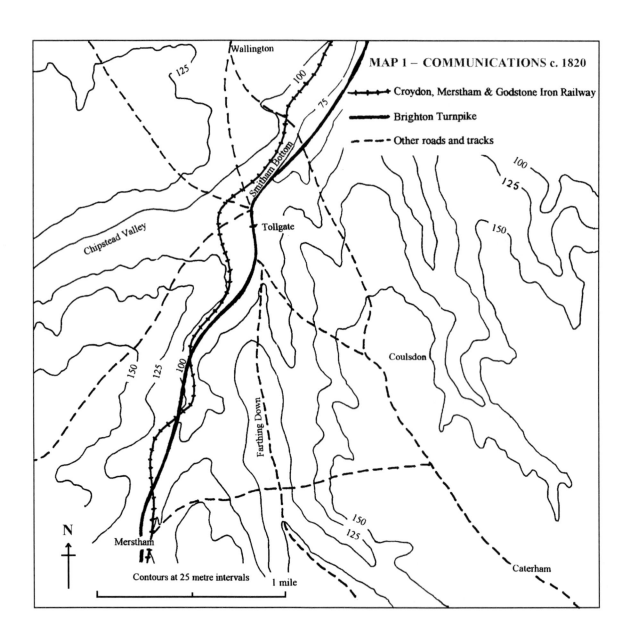

MAP 1 – COMMUNICATIONS c. 1820

Croydon, Merstham & Godstone Iron Railway

Brighton Turnpike

Other roads and tracks

Wallington

Smitham Bottom

Chipstead Valley

Tollgate

Coulsdon

Farthing Down

Caterham

Merstham

N

Contours at 25 metre intervals

1 mile

Chapter 14

Public Transport and Communications

by Bill Gilbert

Before the 19th century there were only a few roads and farm tracks in the Coulsdon area. Two tracks from Caterham to Beddington passed through Coulsdon and across the valley, known as Smitham Bottom, one at Stoats Nest Farm and the other at Lion Green Road. They crossed the road from Croydon to Reigate, which turned along Chipstead Valley before going uphill to Chipstead. Another track led along the valley to Hooley, while an ancient trackway came over Farthing Downs into Smitham Bottom.

THE 19TH CENTURY

On 4 June 1808 a turnpike road from Croydon through Smitham Bottom was opened. It followed the line of the present Brighton Road through Coulsdon, where two milestones can still be seen by the side of the road, one under the railway bridge near Coulsdon South station and the other towards Old Lodge Lane. There was a toll gate near the site of the entrance to Cane Hill Asylum which lasted until 1865 when the tolls were abolished. On the last day a load of wheat was carried from Tollers Farm to Beddington in a cart driven by a nine-year-old boy. Hearing that the toll was being abolished that day, he either spent or lost the money for the return toll and was dismayed to see the gateman on his return. Having no money, he whipped up the horses and drove through at speed. The man threw his lamp at the boy but it fell into his cart. This lamp is now in the possession of the Bourne Society.

Railways

At the beginning of the 19th century the threat to shipping in the Channel posed by the French fleet meant there was every incentive to develop overland links between London and the south coast. Various schemes were put forward, with both canals and horse-drawn railways being considered, following a number of different routes. The eventual choice was for a horse-drawn railway, running initially from Wandsworth to Croydon and the Surrey Iron Railway was the first public railway in the world. Before this railway opened, another line was proposed as the next step to the coast. This was the Croydon, Merstham & Godstone Iron Railway (CMGIR). The line started in Croydon Old Town with a junction from the Surrey Iron Railway and followed the west side of Brighton Road.

At Coulsdon the line crossed Chipstead valley on a viaduct. Part of an embankment, very overgrown, can still be seen at the back of the car park in Lion Green Road, but the horseshoe-shaped bridge over the road has long since been demolished. The line then continued through what are now the grounds of Cane Hill Hospital; the track bed can be seen just to the west of Brighton Road near Hollymeoak Road and again a quarter of a mile further on. It then crossed the Brighton Turnpike to its eastern side. As the line crossed Woodplace Lane the rail, which embodied the flange, was reduced from 3 inches to 1 inch in height, to reduce the impact on road vehicles. An almost-buried bridge over the railway can be observed where it carries Dean Lane over the track. Beyond Hooley the line is now buried below the M23 and then continues in a cutting beside the A23.

The Surrey Iron Railway

A drawing by E F Bishop

The first part of the railway, between Croydon and Merstham, was opened on 24 July 1805. However after Nelson's victory at Trafalgar in October 1805 further extension of the line was abandoned. It was reported that at the opening a train of 12 wagons weighing in all 55 tons was pulled by one horse from Hooley to Croydon, a distance of six miles in under two hours. It should be noted that there was a downhill gradient, but nevertheless this was quite an achievement. The track consisted of flanged cast iron rails 3 feet long, weighing 43½ lbs, mounted on stone blocks with a gauge of 4' 2". A short length of track on its original site survives in Purley Rotary Field.

Owners of goods had to provide their own wagons. These were primitive wooden carts with four wheels, no brakes and a capacity of about three tons. The main types of freight carried were firestone from the Merstham mines, chalk and agricultural produce carried to Croydon for onward transmission to London, and timber, coal and manure to the farms and settlements along the line. About five trucks comprised a train. No passengers were carried and there were no stations. The CMGIR was never successful and the invention of the steam locomotive led to its closure. Eventually it was bought for £9,613.13s.8d by the London & Brighton Railway, which needed to build its line over part of its track.

A passenger railway from London to Brighton was first proposed in 1823, amongst the first in the country. The London & Brighton Railway Co. (LBR) submitted a Bill to Parliament. The South Eastern Railway (SER) also wanted to build its line from London to Dover following roughly the same line as far as Purley, then through the North Downs to Oxted. In 1837 a Parliamentary Commission decided that the SER should start at a junction with the LBR at Redhill and run eastwards to Tonbridge.

Under the Act of Parliament passed on 19 July 1839, the LBR was to build the whole railway between Croydon and Brighton, but was then to sell the section starting half a mile south of Stoats Nest as far as Redhill to the SER. It in turn had to allow the LBR running rights over the track. The six miles between Croydon and Stoats Nest remained the property of the LBR, with the SER retaining running rights over that track. To compound the situation, both Companies had to use the rails belonging to the London & Croydon Railway Company between London Bridge and Croydon! This cumbersome arrangement was to lead to many long and bitter quarrels between the LBR and the SER, the main loser being the travelling public.

Construction of the LBR line began in 1838; it was opened as far as Haywards Heath on 12 July 1841 and to Brighton on 21 September the same year.

The most difficult work was the digging of the very deep cutting that leads from Coulsdon South (not then envisaged as a station) to the start of the tunnel at Merstham. Since the countryside there was practically deserted of habitation, the spoil from this work was dumped beside the line at Smitham Bottom. It was later compacted to form the level ground that can be seen from the bottom of Marlpit Lane and was used as the roadbed for a major locomotive and shunting yard when Coulsdon North was developed. It is now an industrial estate and may well form part of the roadbed for the Coulsdon Relief Road in the near future.

The first station to be built in the area was in 1842, at the point where Stoats Nest Road crosses the line; Stoats Nest was the name given to the station and a level crossing was made at this point. The station was meant to attract racegoers attending the Epsom races eight miles away. Either the railway company was very optimistic or our forefathers were prepared to walk a long way for their pleasures! Either way, the station was unsuccessful and was closed to passengers in 1856. It continued as a goods station until a new station was built about a quarter of a mile further south when the line was quadrupled in 1899. This new station was designed as the terminus for suburban services from London and had four platforms as well as several carriage sidings, a locomotive depot and a goods yard.

As a matter of historical interest, the first station to bear the name Coulsdon was on the Caterham Railway, where Kenley Station was named Coulsdon for the first few months of its life.

The advantages of rail travel over the rough roads of the time gave rise to 'railway mania' in the mid-19th century, resulting in a number of proposals in the Coulsdon area, including—

1860s – London, Chatham & Dover Rly, a line using the London, Brighton & South Coast Railway tracks as far as Stoats Nest, then branching up the Chipstead Valley to Banstead and thence to the Epsom Downs/Sutton line.

1873 – South Caterham Rly, a line from Purley to Old Coulsdon and Upper Caterham along the line of Old Lodge Lane.

1882 – Branch from Coulsdon (Smitham Bottom) via Happy Valley to Upper Caterham.

By 1880 some 70 SER trains and 150 LBSCR trains were using the line daily between Croydon and Redhill. This very heavy traffic led to many problems of timetabling and maintenance of the permanent way, with resultant delays to passengers and several accidents. On 18 July 1877 a LBSCR mail train had been derailed at the old Stoats Nest, resulting in a number of injuries. The Board of Trade enquiry blamed excessive speed and a lack of warning signs to indicate that work was being carried out on the track.

It became obvious that the double line available was insufficient to carry the traffic, so the LBSCR decided to build its own lines paralleling the SER between Croydon and Redhill. The economics of purchasing as little land as possible meant that the track as far south as Smitham Bottom was built by widening the existing right of way from Croydon. Thereafter southwards, to avoid any chance of interference from the SER, the line closely paralleled the SER but at a higher contour where it had to cross over the SER to enter a new tunnel at Merstham. It then reached Redhill, bypassing that station and joining its original road further south. This Quarry Line, as it became known, misses out both the present Coulsdon South and Merstham stations and is now used as the fast Up and Down lines.

During the 1880s there was much building in Coulsdon and in 1883 Cane Hill Asylum was opened. The SER decided to build a station for the use of residents and visitors to the asylum. This station, together with a small goods yard was opened on 1 October 1889 and named Coulsdon. The suffix Cane Hill was added in 1896 and finally the name was changed to Coulsdon South in 1923. The goods yard was closed in 1931.

Just south of where it left the SER track, the Quarry Line entered the grounds of the new Cane Hill Asylum. At the insistence of the Cane Hill Board, what needed only to be a short shallow cutting had to be covered, to reduce the noise and to prevent inmates throwing themselves in front of the trains. So it remained until the cover was removed in 1954.

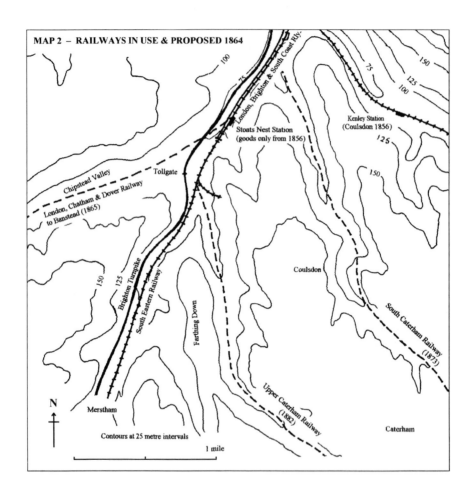

MAP 2 – RAILWAYS IN USE & PROPOSED 1864

In 1890 Cosmo Bonsor, a director of the SER, lived at Kingswood. He became Chairman in 1898. A Chipstead Valley Railway Co had been set up in 1893 and obtained an Act of Parliament that year. Very little happened until 1895, when a scheme was launched to build a light railway to Tadworth along Chipstead Valley and connecting to the Caterham Railway near the junction at Purley. During 1896 consideration was given to building a direct junction with the LBSCR, which was widening the line through Purley – and it would work the line. The junction with the SER had not, however, been completed and the CVR offered to take over the line and complete it. It was built as a single line but bridges were installed to allow for doubling and the gradients were eased, the cost being about £11,000 per mile.

The first section as far as Kingswood was opened on 2 November 1897. The CVR was absorbed by the SER in 1899 and opened as far as Tadworth in 1900 and to Tattenham Corner on Derby Day 1901. The station at Smitham together with a small goods yard was completed in 1904. As an economy measure the station was closed between 1917 and 1919 and the goods yard was axed in the 1960s.

The line has been very popular with racegoers ever since its opening and for many years the Royal train could be seen taking the Royal Family to the Derby.

THE 20TH CENTURY

The 'new' Stoats Nest station was opened by the LBSCR for passenger traffic on 1 April 1900. A few years later, in April 1907, a German film company used the station as a location for a sequence which required an actor to lie across the tracks while a locomotive ground to a halt, stopping just short of him. Unfortunately the Stroudley tank locomotive, No. 379 *Sanderstead*, failed to stop in time and the actor, Mr Zeitz, was killed. The stationmaster, John Bromley, had personally arranged the filming without permission from the railway company and as a result was demoted.

In 1910 a major accident occurred which caused considerable loss of life. On Saturday 29 January of that year, at about 4.30 p.m., the 3.40 express from Brighton to Victoria was derailed when passing through Stoats Nest. The 10-coach train broke in two at the fifth coach, the rear half mounting a platform. Seven people were killed, including William Rose, the manager from Hall & Co's quarry at the bottom of Marlpit Lane, who was crossing the lines at the time and was struck by a falling signal post. Amongst the 42 injured was the wife of Dr Kellett who practised in Coulsdon. They were returning from their honeymoon and Mrs Kellett was taken to Purley Cottage Hospital suffering from severe shock.

The local heroes of this accident and its immediate aftermath were members of the newly-formed 4th Purley Boy Scout Troop. They were playing football on a field at Stoats Nest Farm when they heard the accident. Twelve of them, accompanied by the scoutmaster F H Beckett and his adjutant, Mr Parker, at once set off with their stretcher to aid the wounded. First on the scene, before the medical services, they helped extricate the dead and injured and bore them away to the waiting rooms on the station. A reporter from *The Daily Mirror* later interviewed the heroes, particularly praising the Lion Patrol Leader F Ingrams and Tiger Patrol Leader M Jones for the speed in which they obtained bandages and dressings, which they fetched from their scoutmaster's home nearby. It is worth noting that none of the boys was more than 14 years old at the time. In recognition of this work they were awarded the movement's Medal of Merit.

Following this accident the station was renamed in 1911 to calm passengers' fears, calling it Coulsdon & Smitham Downs (for Cane Hill), although it was still called Stoats Nest on the 1914 6-inch Ordnance Survey map. In 1923 it was called Coulsdon West, then in 1929 it changed names again and became Coulsdon North, which it remained until it was closed in 1984, the locomotive depot having been closed in 1928.

The footbridge across the tracks at Coulsdon North was built to replace an ancient footpath between Old Coulsdon and *The Red Lion*, since 'separating an Englishman from his beer is a serious thing'.

The major change of the new century was the electrification of services, beginning with suburban routes. In 1913 the LBSCR decided to electrify the line from Victoria to Coulsdon & Smitham Downs (Coulsdon North). A year later World War I broke out and work stopped, with electrification only having reached Selhurst.

The power supply to the locomotives was by overhead catenary wire and this was continued when work recommenced in 1922, with the first electric service to Coulsdon North (then Coulsdon West) starting on 1 April 1925. However, following the grouping of the old railway companies in 1923 into the Southern Railway, the new General Manager, Sir Herbert Walker decided to standardise on the third-rail system. Since Victoria – Coulsdon North already had an electric service, the other lines in the district were converted first: the Tattenham Corner line ran its first third-rail electric service on 25 March 1928, with London Bridge to Coulsdon North commencing on 17 June 1928. The last overhead-electric ran from Victoria to Coulsdon North after midnight on 29 September 1929 and the first third-rail service the following morning. The main Brighton line was electrified in 1935.

(Above): Coulsdon North Railway Station in 1928. The station was closed in 1984

Photograph courtesy of Purley Library

(Above): The newly-built Woodmansterne Station, c.1934, looking towards Smitham. It was built to serve the new roads in the western part of the parish – some way from Woodmansterne village

(Left): The two railway bridges at the bottom of Marlpit Lane are shown here in a photograph by F H B Ellis, taken in 1930. The bridge in the distance was rebuilt in 1937

PUBLIC TRANSPORT AND COMMUNICATIONS

On the Tattenham Corner Line a new station called Woodmansterne was opened in 1932 to serve the new housing development in west Coulsdon.

1947 saw the nationalisation of all public transport, and the Southern Railway became the Southern Region of British Rail. Since then, changes have tended to result in the loss of services although the area has managed to keep more than many other places. Despite the 1984 closure of Coulsdon North there are still two stations providing six trains an hour outside rush hours to London, as well as direct services to Gatwick Airport and Brighton, all operated by Connex South Central, which succeeded British Rail Network South East in 1996.

Road Transport

The first motor bus appeared on Brighton Road in 1905, when an ambitious scheme by the Vanguard Company was started for a service from London to Brighton. However an accident to one of the buses at Handcross Hill in Sussex brought about the withdrawal of the service in 1906.

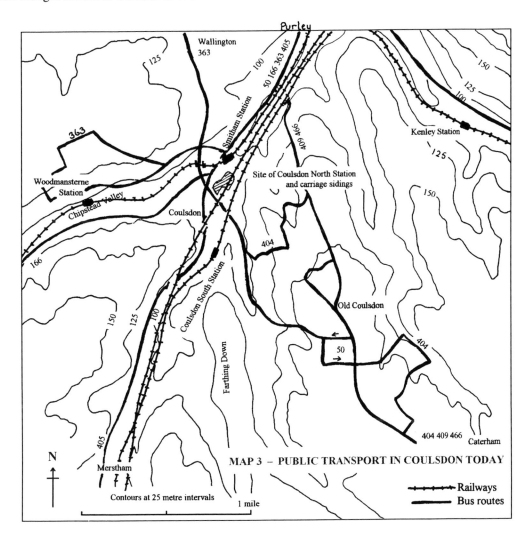

MAP 3 – PUBLIC TRANSPORT IN COULSDON TODAY

(Above): London General Omnibus Company route 58 at *The Red Lion*, Coulsdon, about 1928. Compare this view with the one below, when both *The Red Lion* and the style of buses had been transformed

(Below): A wintry scene in Brighton Road, Coulsdon, taken in the 1930s. The bus in the centre of the photograph is a route 414 on its way to Horsham

PUBLIC TRANSPORT AND COMMUNICATIONS

On 20 July 1913 the London General Omnibus Company (LGOC) started a service from Stockwell to Redhill (No. 116) on Sundays, using the famous red open-topped (B-type) double-decker buses. The route followed the main road and was mainly for the use of Londoners wishing to visit the Surrey countryside. The next year it became a daily service but was diverted to Reigate and renumbered 160. In 1917 it was again renumbered to 59B, and started from Camden Town, but terminated at *The Red Lion* as a wartime economy. With the return of peace the 160 made a brief reappearance, and the 59B was extended again to Reigate. A new company – the East Surrey Traction Co. (ESTC) – started a service from Redhill to Croydon using B-type buses painted blue. This service was numbered S5.

In 1922 the East Surrey Company began a service from Croydon to Chelwood Gate via Stoats Nest Road and Caterham, route S9. This was the first bus to serve Old Coulsdon. At the same time the S5 was extended to Crawley. Both these routes are still in existence through the area as 409 and 405 respectively.

In 1927 a service run by the LGOC began along Chipstead Valley to How Lane. It started from Camden Town and was numbered 58. The following year the ESTC opened an express coach service from Reigate to London along Brighton Road. These coaches were the first to be fitted with pneumatic tyres. The fare to London was 2s.0d single and 3s.0d return. The ESTC was taken over by the LGOC in 1929 and in 1930 the Green Line coaches appeared. These were identified by letters. Those serving Coulsdon were—

E	Bushey to Crawley along the main road
K	Hemel Hempstead to Caterham via Old Coulsdon

In 1933 the London Passenger Transport Board took over all bus and tram routes in London . This resulted in another reorganisation; bus routes in Coulsdon at this time were—

Green Line Coaches:	G	London – Caterham via Old Coulsdon;	I	Abbots Langley – Crawley
LPTB buses	58	Camden Town – Chipstead Valley;	59	Camden Town – Reigate
	405	Croydon – Crawley;	409	Croydon – Forest Row
	414	Croydon – Horsham		

Later the 58 was renumbered 59, which was withdrawn from Reigate and a new service – 411 – was introduced between Croydon and Reigate travelling through Old Coulsdon and Caterham. This was subsequently diverted to run through Coulsdon and up Marlpit Lane to Caterham. The route was cut in the 1970s, made a brief reappearance as the 400, and is now the 466, terminating at Caterham.

With the growth of Old Coulsdon in the 1930s more buses were needed; few people had cars at that time. In 1939 another new route started from Croydon to Coulsdon, up Marlpit Lane and Mead Way to terminate at *The Tudor Rose*. Like all other routes it has changed number frequently – 190, 50, and now 60.

On the outbreak of World War II all Green Line coaches were withdrawn and later – as an economy measure – all Sunday morning bus services were stopped. The Green Line coaches returned in 1946 as routes 709 and 710. Public transport was nationalised in 1947, when the LPTB became the London Transport Executive, but there were no practical changes.

The next change was the start of a local service in 1957 serving the Clock House Farm estate on Saturday only, to enable residents to shop in Coulsdon. This was run by Banstead Coaches from 1964 and then with deregulation, the East Surrey Co. reappeared and took it over until 1995 when Epsom Buses obtained the franchise. It is now run as a daily service (363) and has been extended to Croydon in one direction and Wallington in the other.

Following deregulation a totally new service opened between Croydon and Epsom via Coulsdon, the No. 498, also run by Epsom Buses. This follows the route of the old 59, which had been renumbered 166 terminating at *The Midday Sun*. The new service has now become the 166 throughout, with one bus an hour continuing to Epsom via Banstead.

In 1995 another local route, No. 404, opened. This shuttles between Coulsdon and Caterham, following a complicated route to reach the shopping areas of Coulsdon and Old Coulsdon.

A novel method of transport

**– Miss Florence, the American Globe Walker,
passing Smitham Bottom on 19 June 1903, on her
way to Brighton**

**The photograph was taken in Brighton Road, near
its junction with Marlpit Lane**

Chapter 15

Farms & Farming from the mid 19th Century

by Eric W Groves

The terrain of the Coulsdon district with its ridges of chalk sloping northwards towards Brighton Road and Purley has been likened to a four-pronged fork, the ridges being the tines and the deeply dissecting valleys the spaces in between. Old Coulsdon lies to the south on a flat plateau where the soil varies from calcareous loam to patches of clay with flints overlying the chalk.

Eight of the 12 farms enumerated later in the account were situated on this plateau, two on the ridge slopes and two in the valleys in between. Few ponds occurred either on the ridges or on the plateau, and most farms sank their own wells, which on the top meant drilling down 200-300 feet before permanent water was reached.

The calcareous loam and clay-with-flints over the chalk, while producing satisfactory crops, was difficult to cultivate, as ploughing brought up flint nodules and these had to be cleared. Farmers hired casual labour, both men and women, to pick up the flints by hand and stack them at the side of the fields ready for removal in carts. Both Godstone and Croydon authorities accepted loads of these flints, which were broken up and rammed into muddy, unmetalled roads to provide a better surface for the wintertime.

Coulsdon's farms were not large by today's standards, most being under 200 acres. They were mixed farms i.e. both arable and livestock, growing various crops and raising mostly sheep and cattle. Of the former, wheat for human consumption was the most important, while oats and roots were grown for animal food. Hay was cut and stacked to provide additional food for cattle and horses.

Livestock

Of the livestock, Southdown sheep were by far the largest group of animals raised; not so much for wool (though this was of significance) but more especially for their meat which by the 19th century was required to supply the ever-growing population of towns.

An early engraving of a Southdown ewe and lamb. The breed today is smaller, fatter and has finer wool

Eventide, Coulsdon.   G&E.Laister.

**A shepherd brings his flock along the lane (now Downs Road). The
sheep had been grazing on the slopes of Farthing Downs**

Throughout spring, summer and autumn sheep were kept on the open downland in the charge of a shepherd, the flocks being moved to fresh pasturage from time to time. In winter they were brought nearer to the homestead and turned out onto the stubble left from the previous season's harvest, to which hay or roots were brought by a farmhand. Here they could feed while at the same time dunging the field ready to be ploughed for the next year's crop. Alternatively they might be driven onto a field on which there were the remnants of a root crop such as turnips. To prevent wasteful feeding and undue trampling, the sheep would be penned inside a moveable wattle or hurdle fencing. The shepherd, with perhaps the help of a boy, would move this fencing a short way each day.

The Croydon livestock market in Selsdon Road was built in 1848, so then the sheep from Coulsdon farms were driven along Brighton Road, through Purley and South Croydon for sale there and subsequent slaughter. Although the breed most commonly found on the farms was the Southdown there were a few flocks of Hampshire Down sheep too.

Of the cattle, the most frequently kept were the Frisian and the Dairy Shorthorn. During the latter part of the 19th century the yearly milk yield had been greatly increased by an improved knowledge of selective breeding and scientific feeding. The cows would be taken from their stalls after early morning milking and driven out to pasture fields. They would not be brought back until late afternoon, when they would be milked again before being bedded down on straw for the night.

Milking in those days was done by hand, for a practical milking machine was not invented until 1895. Most of the milk was sold to local dairies for delivery to local residents. Bullocks that were being raised for beef were kept within the homestead byres on straw. They were fed on roots, chaff, cattle cake and hay.

FARMS & FARMING FROM THE MID 19TH CENTURY

A small herd of pigs was kept on some farms, the usual breeds in north east Surrey being the Surrey or the Berkshire. Poultry-keeping was not on any commercial scale, but all farms had a few chickens which were usually under the care of the farmer's wife. They were raised essentially for the family's needs though surplus eggs might occasionally be sold at the farm gate. Light Sussex and Rhode Island Red were two breeds favoured, the former being considered a good layer. The Dorking fowl (unusual in having five-clawed feet) was kept as a capon to fatten up for Christmas.

Arable Land

Turning now to arable crops that were raised on Coulsdon farms, roots such as turnips, swedes and mangolds were grown for winter feed for cattle and sheep. Rape and kale were occasionally planted mainly for feeding the ewes after lambing. Sainfoin and clover were often added when re-sowing grasses in pasture fields in order to increase the nutrient value of the hay, particularly essential to provide energy for the horses which were the farms' sole source of haulage power right up until after World War II.

It is as well at this point briefly to describe the annual cycle of wheat-growing and harvesting, as it was practised on most of the farms in the area.

After the harvest of one year had been gathered in, the land would be ploughed between late September and December. From the beginning of the 19th century various types of plough were introduced, the best suited to land on chalk hills being the Kentish turnwrest (so called as it turns over the furrows in one direction). Heavy horses were required to pull it, varying between a pair and up to six according to how full the soil was with flints. After rolling and harrowing, sowing followed and the seed was broadcast by hand, a method adopted since early man and still in use on at least one farm in north east Surrey up to the 1930s. However most farms by the mid-19th century had progressed to using a horse-drawn drill.

Throughout the following spring and summer the grain germinated, the stalk developed and the ears at the top containing the corn ripened. Some time in August or September a field would be ready for harvesting, a process which involved almost all the farm's workforce, plus as many other local folk that could lend a hand, both men and women.

Harvesting near Coulsdon North Station

10 August 1954

Photograph courtesy of Purley Library

Page 113

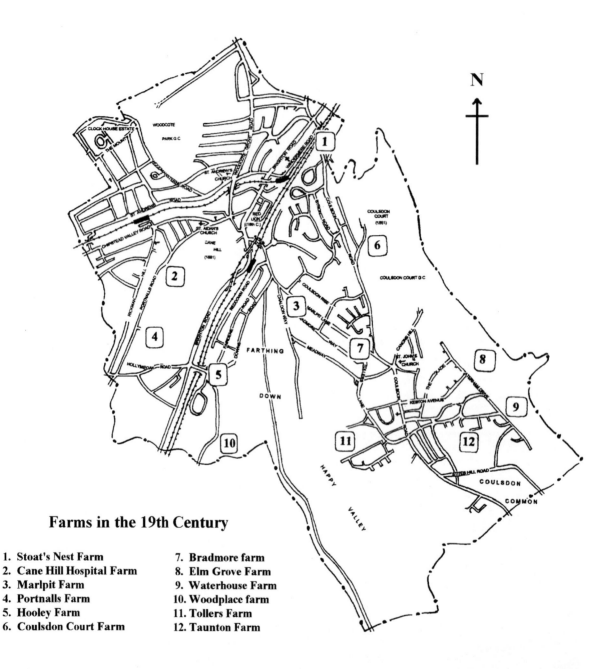

Farms in the 19th Century

1. Stoat's Nest Farm
2. Cane Hill Hospital Farm
3. Marlpit Farm
4. Portnalls Farm
5. Hooley Farm
6. Coulsdon Court Farm
7. Bradmore farm
8. Elm Grove Farm
9. Waterhouse Farm
10. Woodplace farm
11. Tollers Farm
12. Taunton Farm

FARMS & FARMING FROM THE MID 19TH CENTURY

Since Saxon times it had been the practice for the reapers (men) to move forward in a line towards the standing crop, each with his sickle and, grasping a handful of stalks, sometimes with the help of a stick, would cut them low down near the ground. Following the reapers there would be another line of workers (women and perhaps older children) who would gather the stalks into armfuls, tie them into sheaves. These sheaves would be grouped to dry, usually four or five bundles in each, known as stooks. The stooks would be left standing in the field for a few days to complete the drying process, when they would be loaded onto carts and brought back to the homestead to be stored in the farm's largest barn.

Harvesting was hard work and very labour intensive, so it was not surprising that during the 19th century a mechanical reaping machine became available. This was drawn by horses at first, but in the 20th century by tractors. Such machines were not however seen on farms in north-east Surrey until later than the rest of the county. From the 1880s onwards this machine and its successor, the reaper-binder, greatly reduced the labour required at harvest.

The introduction of machines to harvesting was not met without resentment among the farm workers, as it meant a loss of earnings for the major breadwinner which would be felt during the winter. These early machines, however, still left quite a number of headed stalks uncut or lying on the ground. The farmer usually permitted nearby villagers, both women and children, to glean as many stalks as they were able. This provided a welcome addition to the family's needs, for a bag of corn could be exchanged by the local miller for its equivalent weight in flour.

The gathered sheaves stored in the farmstead barn would remain for a while until they could be threshed. During the 18th and 19th centuries it was a wintertime task for the men to thresh it with the use of a wooden flail. They would separate the grain from the heads by bringing the heavy jointed part of the flail onto the stalks spread out on the tiled part of the barn floor. By the second half of the 19th century improved mechanical threshing machines became increasingly available, which eliminated the laborious hand flailing. Nevertheless even these new threshers, driven by a belt from a steam traction engine, still involved 15 or more workers. Not only did such machines separate and pass the grain into sacks, but in later models they also transported the straw up an elevator so that men could build it into stacks or ricks.

The combine harvester did not become available until after World War II, by which time most of Coulsdon's farms were no more.

1.   STOATS NEST FARM

A farm had been on the Stoats Nest site since 1688, when it was owned by the Bouverie family and was later occupied by a succession of tenant farmers. On the 1762 Messeder map it is shown as Stoats Nest and it was also referred to as 'The Old Brew House' – the farmer at

Stoats Nest Farmhouse that formerly stood at the junction of Stoats Nest Road and Brighton Road. Photographed 1908 by M G Sharp

Demolished c.1910

Courtesy of Purley Library

the time brewed ale as well as raising crops. In 1785 it already had the double row of elms depicted on the Bainbridge map on its Brighton Road frontage and remembered into the 20th century. In 1800 it was 180 acres in size and about 20 years later the farm's size had by then been reduced to 51 acres.

In 1837 it was owned by Thomas Byron and tenanted by Charles Bleaden and later, in 1851 by Richard Bashford. The last tenant farmer was William Hoare, but after he left the farmhouse itself fell into decay and was demolished about 1910. A few of the outbuildings remained for some years afterwards, one barn being used during World War I as a rifle range. Edgar Hobden, who provided horse cabs at the second Stoats Nest station (later to be named Coulsdon North) and also a brake to take cricket and football teams to away matches, stabled his horses and vehicles in one of the old barns. Another, pulled down in 1916, had some of its ragstones incorporated into Coulsdon's first Roman Catholic Church which stood on Woodcote Grove Road near the junction with Chipstead Valley Road. The premises subsequently became the Co-Operative Hall and in the 1990s became a centre for the martial arts. These fragments of history of the old Stoats Nest Farm are still visible.

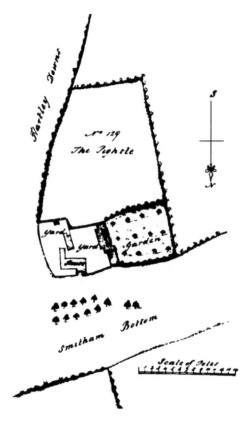

Plan of Stoats Nest Farm from the Messeder Field Book 1762
Courtesy of Purley Library

2.   CANE HILL HOSPITAL FARM

Cane Hill Hospital was built between 1878 and 1883 on land purchased from the Portnalls estate. Its associated farm was created in order to make the hospital self-sufficient. Some of the patients helped with the farm work.

D A Bayliss has given an interesting account of the farm. Initially hay was harvested, but later potatoes, cabbage, coleworts (rape and colza) and turnips were also planted. Pigs were introduced to consume the food-waste from the hospital itself.

The farm buildings consisted of the farmhouse (originally built for the farm bailiff), pigsties, and suitable housing for the cattle. This last was set round a courtyard and was equipped with Musgrove Patent cast-iron cow stalls – an innovation for the time.

The farm ceased to function as such during the 1960s, the outbuildings being turned over to use as riding stables.

3.   MARLPIT FARM

The site of this farm, which lay on the south side of Marlpit Lane, was not represented on the map until the Ordnance Survey 6-inch 1914 edition. Oddly it was not shown on the previous edition on the same scale published in 1897, although the flint-walled construction of the farmhouse (surviving today as a private residence at No. 22 Marlpit Lane) has a date set in stone of 1878. It remained the only building on the hillside of the lane until after World War I when housing development began in this area. What had formerly been a narrow rutted track became, within a few years, a wide metalled road.

Sketch of Marlpit Farm and its outbuildings by M Ramage, 1920. Now only the house – as a private residence – remains
Courtesy of Purley Library

(Below): **Portnalls Farm. 1915.**
Courtesy of Purley Library.

A J Keeble was the farmer at Marlpit Farm in 1906 when future local historian Una Broadbent came to live with her parents in Downs Road. She remarks that his sheep were regularly grazed on the downs, attended by a shepherd and that the flock wore bells around their necks.

In Purley Reference Library there exists a coloured sketch made in 1920 by M E Ramage, of the farmhouse and its outlying barns. It is not known when the farm ceased operating, although it was probably in the late 1920s, when the land was sold for housing when Bradmore Way, Mead Way and Chaldon Way were laid out.

4. PORTNALLS FARM

The first reference to a farm at Portnalls is in 1362, and it was amongst the lands restored to Sir Francis Carew by Queen Mary Tudor in 1554, when it brought in £6.13s.4d per annum. Later mentions occur in several court rolls between the years 1654 and 1738. In 1762 the whole of the Portnalls estate, owned by Sir John Stanley and rented to Mrs Eliza Wood, reportedly amounted to 362 acres but thereafter its size diminished. In 1786 it was owned and occupied by John Hilbert Esquire implying that it had become a country gentleman's

house. By 1800 the farm itself was reduced to 186 acres. The following year its position was shown on John Cary's Surrey map. Thomas Byron I bought the estate in 1837, moving there from Hooley House when part of the Hooley land was purchased by the London & Brighton Railway Co. The Byrons moved from Portnalls when their new house at Hartley Farm (Coulsdon Court) was completed in 1850.

Portnalls was still farmed with Joseph Tucker as the last tenant farmer. He is remembered for having diverted Portnalls Road in 1873 to its present position 'from another further east' and also 'laid out Rickman Hill on the line of a former footpath'. The present Portnalls was built in the 1880s. The last relic of the old house – a vast barn, 100 feet by over 40, framed in oak and chestnut, with flint and brick filling – was demolished in 1939 and the almost indestructible beams used to fill in a well.

The whole estate was sold to London County Council and Cane Hill Hospital was built. Thereafter the farm lands were worked as the Hospital home farm until the 1960s and the Hospital itself was closed in 1992.

5.   HOOLEY HOUSE FARM

The only reference to this farm so far traced is that it was attached to Hooley House, but 'was destroyed when the Netherlands Estate in Coulsdon was developed'. It may be the one of this name mentioned in 1203. The name 'Hooley Farm', found on modern maps some distance further south than the site of the old Hooley House estate, is not in any way connected with the former farm of the same name. During the daytime the sheep of Hooley House Farm were grazed on the slopes of Farthing Downs.

6.   COULSDON COURT FARM

In 1850 Thomas Byron III pulled down the farmhouse of Hartley Farm and built a grander residence on the same site which he later called Coulsdon Court. The former Coulsdon Court, next to St John's Church was renamed The Grange, since it no longer fulfilled the task of housing the local court. The farmlands belonging to the new Coulsdon Court were restyled Coulsdon Court Farm, but it is difficult to establish its actual size at that time. It is quoted as 1000 acres by Frank Leeson, but this figure obviously included land from Stoats Nest and Bradmore Farms which had also been absorbed into the Byron estate.

A new farm using the old name of Hartley Farm was established on land between the present Hartley Down, where the squire's warren used to be, and Old Lodge Lane. Details of this farm are in the Bourne Society's book *Village Histories: 1. Purley.*

After the death in 1921 of Edmund, the last Byron to be squire of Coulsdon, the whole estate was broken up and sold for development. Coulsdon Court house and its parkland became a golf clubhouse and golf course; now the house, much added to, is the Coulsdon Manor Hotel, with the golf clubhouse and a sports centre in its grounds.

The farmlands were partitioned and auctioned as building plots. Today just about all of it that is outside the protection of the Green Belt has been developed into housing.

7.   BRADMORE FARM

Bradmore Farm was the successor in name to the earlier Colgrime's Farm, so-called after the manorial tenant Colgrimes (or Colgryms), a family name that persisted in Coulsdon for over 400 years. The Bainbridge Map of 1785 still referred to it as Colgrime's farm. The Georgian exterior is misleading. It is an 18th century extension to an older, timber-framed house. This is apparent when you enter. The main door leads straight into the added front room and the original exterior wall is facing you. Nearby Bradmore pond had at one time provided an important source of water for the local villagers and their livestock.

8. ELM GROVE FARM

This name is marked on modern maps, but no information so far has been traced as to its original extent nor any names of past tenant farmers. It appears to have been, probably early in the 19th century, a secondary farm to Bradmore Farm (Colgrime's).

9. WATERHOUSE FARM

Messeder in his survey of Coulsdon Farms in 1762 gives Henry Rowed as the owner of Waterhouse Farm and shows its position on his map. In 1886 J Budgen was the tenant farmer. W Martingell recalls that as a boy around the turn of the last century, this farm 'stretched from the present Kenley Aerodrome to *The Wattenden Arms*. It had a very good well and other farmers used to go there for water if their own wells ran dry. Mr Weedon was the farmer at that time and grew mangolds and wheat, and kept cows, chickens and sheep'. The farm land was worked until about 1930 and the farmhouse itself, which stood off Hayes Lane, was said to have been demolished during World War II.

10. WOODPLACE FARM

The land of this farm was situated near the foot of the downland ridge west of Farthing Downs. It lay near one of the earliest sites occupied by Coulsdon man, where pottery remains of the Romano-British period have been found.

A sale catalogue of 29 September 1823 announced an auction from the farm of livestock consisting of 572 head of Southdown lambs, ewes and rams; one bull, 15 heifers, one calf and two cart horses, all the property of Revd William J Jolliffe.

Woodplace Farm to the west of Farthing Downs.

Before 1908

Courtesy Croydon Local Studies Library

In 1837 it was 268 acres in extent and farmed by Alexander Oades, but by 1851 it was down to 226 acres and occupied by William Brown. When it was put up for sale in 1979 it had been further reduced to 177 acres. The original timber-framed farmhouse with its brick in-filling was demolished during World War II but a wing that had been added later remains as the present dwelling. The land belonging to Woodplace Farm was cultivated until the 1970s by patients from Netherne Hospital.

11. TOLLERS FARM

This farm is said to have been named after the Toller family in the 14th century. This was a trade name, used by a man who either collected tolls (on behalf of Chertsey Abbey?), or who tolled the bell in the church or at

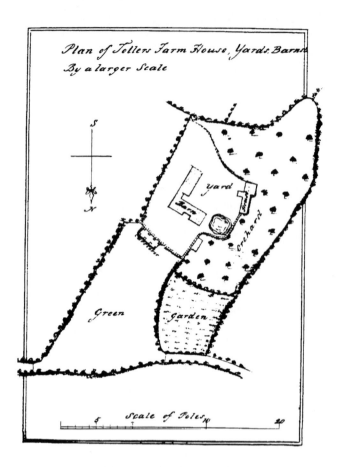

Plan of Tollers Farm from the Messeder Field Book 1762. The old farmhouse was burnt down in 1935. The present house is a private dwelling

Courtesy of Purley Library

curfew. It was surveyed in 1762 when it was 245 acres and held at that time by Thomas Winch. By 1837 the land had become part of Thomas Byron's estate, the tenant farmer being Abraham Brown. The size had risen to 350 acres and by 1851 when it was occupied by James Brown it had been further increased to 400 acres, with a labour force of 20. In 1865 J Budgen was tenant and he also later farmed Waterhouse Farm. Between 1920 and 1927 Tollers Farm was occupied by Alfred Moule and from 1939 to 1945 by G Ashwood.

The old farmhouse was burnt down in 1935. The present house, now a private dwelling, was converted and enlarged from a former barn. Pigs were still raised until the early 1980s but the building in which they had been housed has now become the Tollers Design Centre.

12.   TAUNTON FARM

Taunton Farmhouse is purported to be the oldest secular building in Coulsdon and formed the Manor House of Taunton, with records going back to 1191. Its position is shown on the Messeder map of 1762.

For over 20 years from 1826 the farm and its two associated windmills were held by the Russell family. During that period they made several attempts to sell by auction. This however was not achieved (at least for the farm itself) until 1849; then the two windmills failed to reach the reserve price and were withdrawn from auction. George Hoare had a 14 year lease as tenant farmer from October 1848 and in the Census of 1851 the size of the farm was given as 112 acres. Unlike most other farms in the Coulsdon area, Taunton Farm never became part of the Byron family estate.

Taunton Farm, a listed building, photographed in 1928 by F H B Ellis, now a private house

Courtesy of Purley Library

Thomas Edward Couling had been tenant for a number of years up until his death in 1918. Taunton Farm ceased to be actively engaged in agriculture soon after this.

The farmhouse, now a private residence, is of a flint and brick construction with a tile-hung exterior, but inside the main part of the house shows evidence of being originally a 15th century open hall with a three-bay crossing.

SOURCES

Anon (*c.*1980s) *The History of Old Coulsdon.* (Local History Pack, Croydon Public Libraries)

Anon. *Coulsdon and Old Coulsdon.* (Local History Packs, Croydon Libraries, Museum & Arts)

Auction schedule of Messrs. Blake of Cornhill, London, 30 November 1849

Bourne Society *Local History Records* and Bulletins

BROADBENT, U & LATHAM, R. (eds) (1976) *Coulsdon – Downland Village.* Bourne Society

FUSSELL, G E (1981) *The Farmers' Tools.* London

GRIGG, D (1989) *English Agriculture; an historical perspective.* Oxford

HALL, A D & RUSSELL, E J (1911) *A Report on the Agriculture and Soils of Kent, Surrey & Sussex* London.

Historical note prepared by George Trollope & Sons, Belgrave Square, London, for their sale particulars of Tollers Farm. n.d. (*c.*1967)

LAZENBY, F (1964) *Village Days in Old Coulsdon.* St John's Parish Church Magazine Jan- Dec. 1964

MALDEN, H E (1902-1912) *Victoria County History: Surrey*

MESSEDER, Isaac (1762) Field Book & Accompanying Map

Sale Catalogue in the Hylton mss, Somerset Record Office. (see PRINGLE, C. Bourne Society Bulletin 102, 1980, p 8)

SHORT, M E (*c*1973) *Coulsdon & Smitham Bottom* Croydon Primary Curriculum Development Unit.

THARBY, W G (1972) *The History of Coulsdon West.* Coulsdon West Residents' Association

WARD'S *Commercial & General Croydon Directories*

Installing telephone lines in Wilhemina Avenue, August 1956.

Courtesy of Croydon Local Studies Library.

Chapter 16

Public Services and Industry

by Bill Gilbert

SERVICES

Telephones

There was a manual telephone exchange in operation in Croydon in 1884, but there are no records showing the first installation of a telephone in Coulsdon. However, Hall & Company had a telephone at its Marlpit Lane works in 1890 which was probably connected to the Croydon exchange.

In the early years of the 20th century the use of telephones was starting to spread in business and among the upper and middle classes. By 1904 there were 771 subscribers to the Croydon exchange and on 1 November 1911 a new exchange was opened at 2 Elm Cottages, Merstham with 43 lines. This exchange moved to new premises at Station Approach, Merstham in 1927 using CB 10 (battery operated) equipment and three years later a new exchange named Downland (now part of the 01737 group) was instituted and moved to its present building in Hollymeoak Road on 29 July 1930 with 143 subscribers. Downland remained as a manual exchange until the mid 1960s.

The other exchange serving the Coulsdon area in the early days was housed in Purley at the exchange opened in 1910 in a shop in Mafeking Terrace. In 1914 it moved to purpose-built premises in Purley High Street where it remained until new larger premises were built in Brighton Road near the Council Offices in 1931. On 15 July 1935 the exchange name was changed from Purley to Uplands. On 21 July 1954 new equipment was introduced making it an auto-manual exchange. It became an STD exchange on 22 April 1964.

The rapid growth of telephone use was foreseen shortly before World War II and a memo of July 1939 forecast that another exchange would be needed to serve the growing population of Coulsdon and Purley. Unfortunately the war, and reconstruction afterwards (the Downlands exchange was damaged by bombing in 1940) prevented any further growth until 1958 when the Bywood exchange began operating, sharing the Uplands building. In 1970 the use of exchange names was dropped and replaced by numbers, Uplands becoming 660 and Bywood 668. Since then, advances in technology have allowed more users to be accommodated in the same premises and exchanges to be grouped. Mobile telephones use central installations, and the only signs of their use is the ever-growing number of aerial masts sprouting on hilltops and other open spaces.

Water Supply

Until the latter part of the 19th century the residents of Coulsdon had to rely on wells and ponds for all their water. There was a pond at Bradmore Green, which is still there today, and another, Lacey Pond, which was 14ft deep and was the scene of a fatal acident in 1890 when a dog cart ran into it. The driver and his niece were saved but the girl's mother and brother drowned. A third pond was on Coulsdon Common – this was paid for by two Kerrill sisters in 1834 and known as Sisters' Pond. In the valley at Smitham Bottom there was a pond near *The Red Lion* on Lion Green, but this became polluted and was built over in 1880. There were many other field and farm ponds in the parish.

Mains water was first supplied to Coulsdon sometime between 1869 and 1881. In 1859 a speculative builder in Caterham decided to supply piped water to the houses he was building. However he found it too expensive and sold the plant to a group of businessmen who founded the Caterham Spring Water Company. The company received permission by Act of Parliament in 1862 to supply water to surrounding parishes including Coulsdon. Another company, the Kenley Waterworks Company, was formed in 1869, with operations based on wells near Kenley Station. With a plentiful supply it began to pipe water to those parts of Coulsdon parish near its works. In 1885 the two companies combined to form the East Surrey Water Company, which gradually extended its area of supply. By 1896 more reserves were needed, and authority was obtained to build a new works at Purley. Demand for water continued to grow as the population increased and the East Surrey Water Act of 1921 provided for the construction of a well and a pumping station at Smitham, next to *The Red Lion*. This borehole is still in use although the pumping station has been demolished and an office block built on the site. The well and pumping station were completed in 1936. The water was piped to the works at Purley for treatment until it closed in 1988.

Brighton Road pumping station and the library, looking southwards from outside *The Red Lion*, 1936

Courtesy of Croydon Local Studies Library

Also in the 1860s, Sutton & Cheam Water Company began to supply water to Sutton, and its area also expanded to cover the parishes of Beddington and Woodmansterne, which included Chipstead Valley and west Coulsdon. Just before World War II the Sutton and District Water Company completed a water treatment plant in Chipstead Valley, and in 1996 it amalgamated with East Surrey Water Company. Following the merger new mains were laid along Chipstead Valley Road, allowing water to flow between the two companies' networks. Originally mains were made of cast iron and have lasted for nearly a century, but recently they have begun to deteriorate, resulting in many leaks. The newly-formed company has undertaken a programme of replacing the old cast iron mains with concrete or plastic pipes.

Gas

In 1866 the Croydon Commercial Gas & Coke Company was empowered by Parliament to supply the parish of Coulsdon. In 1904 the company's name changed to the Croydon Gas Company, and in 1949 on nationalisation it became part of the South Eastern Gas Board. In 1887 Caterham & District Gaslight & Coke Company was authorised to supply parts of Coulsdon parish with gas, but these areas are now outside the modern district of Coulsdon.

By 1895 there were 12 gas lamps lighting the streets of Coulsdon – this had increased to 76 plus one oil lamp at Stoats Nest by 1902.

PUBLIC SERVICES AND INDUSTRY

Electricity

Electricity for domestic use in Coulsdon began to appear in the early 1900s. The County of London Electric Supply Company, whose generating station was at Wandsworth, obtained an Act of Parliament in 1905 to increase its area of operations, and the Croydon Rural Electric Lighting Order of that year authorised the laying of cables in Coulsdon parish. Roads named for supply included Brighton, Edward, Victoria, Fairdene and Red Down Roads; also the road crossing the S.E. Railway at Chipstead Valley (later Woodcote Grove Road). There is no mention of Old Coulsdon. A report of the Coulsdon parish meeting of July 1905 records that £700 was voted for the lighting of streets in Coulsdon but without naming them. Even as late as 1921 there was neither electricity nor gas in Coulsdon Road.

Before the County of London Electric Supply Company obtained its Act there had been interest by the Corporation of Croydon in supplying electricity to the area but this was unsuccessful. The County of London Electric Supply Company remained the supplier until nationalisation in 1948.

Police

Law enforcement was the responsibility of the parish until the establishment of the Metropolitan Police. The last parish constable was Joseph Nash and the last Coulsdon court was held in 1861, the year that the Metropolitan Police District was extended to include Coulsdon. At that time the area of the Metropolitan Police was extended to include all land within the zone encircled by the City of London 'coal posts'.

Albert Dyer, who was a policeman in the 1920s, recalled that there was a police box with a blue flashing light outside *The Red Lion* in Brighton Road, and as he lived opposite he was often called upon to answer it. He also remembers pushing drunks in a barrow to the police station at Kenley, unless they were locals, when they were either taken home or put in the garden at the back of Downside Pharmacy to sleep it off! Other prisoners were taken by bus to the police station at Kenley.

Fire Service

In 1896 Coulsdon Parish Council resolved to establish a fire service. This was composed of a volunteer force of six men with a horse-drawn engine, stationed at Purley in one of the arches below the railway. The horse was lent by Markwick the butcher of Purley. Difficulties arose if a fire was near the boundary of Croydon because Croydon water hydrants were of a different type and the hoses did not fit.

After the establishment of the Coulsdon & Purley UDC it was decided to purchase a motor fire engine for £1,000. A demonstration was arranged using water from the pond at Bradmore Green, but unfortunately when the hoses were connected to the motorised pump the pressure burst them! Nevertheless the new engine was bought.

Libraries

A parish lending library was set up at Purley in 1899 and a branch opened at Smitham Bottom in 1902. The service was later taken over by Surrey County Council and books were issued from schools. The service was very restricted – Smitham was open to adults for 1½ hours a week and Chipstead Valley for half an hour. By 1934 SCC decided to ask the district councils if they wanted to take over the library service – Coulsdon & Purley voted to do this in November 1934 and raised a rate of 2d in the pound (£4400) to pay for running the service including staff. It was decided to build five libraries to serve the council area – at Purley, Coulsdon, Sanderstead, Kenley and Selsdon. Work on all the buildings began and all five were ready and opened on 25 May 1936 – quite an achievement. The library at Bradmore Green was not opened until 1963.

Post Office

There was a post office in Coulsdon from at least the middle of the 19th century. The 1851 census records that the post office was at Bradmore Green and the postmistress was Judith Hurrell. By 1891 there was another post office at Smitham Bottom at the junction of Brighton Road and Chipstead Valley Road. The postmaster was Henry Wells. About 1910, at the time that the postal address was changed to Coulsdon and the village at the top of the hill became Old Coulsdon, the post office was moved to the shop in Brighton Road opposite the library. The post office was moved to its present position in Chipstead Valley Road in 1935.

(Right): **1. Cherry Tree Cottage, former post office, beer-house and general store**

Coulsdon Post Offices

(Left): **2. The post office next to St John's Church, 1931**

Photograph by F H B Ellis

Courtesy of Purley Library

(Right): **3. The post office in Brighton Road, opposite the library About 1910**

Coulsdon Post Offices

4. The present Coulsdon Post Office in Chipstead Valley Road, which opened in 1935

Photographed in 2000

INDUSTRY

Until the coming of the railway, industries were limited to those found in all agricultural communities – blacksmiths, wheelwrights, millers and other small industries.

In 1862 Hall Brothers, who operated the **quarry** at Merstham, took a lease on land at Coulsdon called Ridlam Bottom and Old Peter's Three Score Acres. These were arable fields belonging to the Byron family. They were probably attractive to Halls because of the chalk just below the surface, and the proximity of the railway line. Branch lines and sidings were quickly added to facilitate the shipment of the quarried materials. In 1864 lime-burning began at the new works. The lease at Merstham having expired Coulsdon became Hall Brothers' major quarry and thus began the huge excavation which is now the Ullswater Industrial Estate.

Chalk was the *raison d'être,* but a useful addition was the flints which were sold to pottery manufacturers as a source of silica. The chalk was either burnt on site to produce lime for use in making mortar or was sent by rail to cement works. By 1903 over 13,000

C E Cook driving the locomotive of a train of skip wagons at Coulsdon Lime Works 1948
From Dobson, C G (1951) *A Century and a Quarter*

Hall & Co's chalk pit, early 1950s

Photograph courtesy of Norman Hurst

(Below):

Disused lime kiln at Coulsdon – "The Old End 'Un" – a document store during World War II

From Dobson C G (1951) *A Century and a Quarter*

tons of chalk were being sent each year by rail from Coulsdon to Halls' cement works at Beddington. This was in addition to the chalk being burnt at Coulsdon to produce lime.

In January 1910 Mr Rose, the manager at Marlpit Lane, was waiting on the platform at Stoats Nest when a train left the track as it passed through the station and he was one of the fatalities of the accident .

New plant for making hydrated lime (Priest kilns) was introduced in 1937 and production continued, with only a short break in 1944 when a flying bomb put the works out of action, until the early 1960s when quarrying ceased and the derelict land was offered for redevelopment. Some of the old kilns resisted all attempts at demolition – even the Army using explosives failed to destroy them. Gradually the land was cleared and new roads and warehouses built over the old quarry floor. There are now upwards of 30 firms, varying from frozen food to telecommunications, occupying the area.

One of the traditional industries was the **wheelwright's** run by the Rivers family on Coulsdon Common from the early 19th

Century until about 1952. Latterly it made wheelbarrows and other garden implements. Tom Rivers died in 1967, and the shop was demolished in 1969.

The Wheelwright's Shop, Stites Hill Road

A Oliver at work

1925

Photograph courtesy of Croydon Local Studies Library

Tom Rivers' Wheelwright's Shop on Coulsdon Common

1940

Photograph courtesy of Croydon Local Studies Library

The 1871 census records Alfred Gilbert as a **miller** on Coulsdon Common. There were two windmills – both post mills – on the common. The first record of a mill is on Rocque's map of 1764 when it was shown as a freehold mill with Taunton Farm. The second was said to have been built in 1777 and stood on an enclosure of the common leased from the lord of the manor for 5s.0d per annum. Richard Dewdney owned the mills from 1780 to 1800; his son James until 1826. Richard Russell owned the mills until 1861. In 1846 and 1849 unsuccessful attempts had been made to sell both. After modernisation, including installing patent

The Windmill on Coulsdon Common

Watercolour by W W Acock, 1910

Courtesy of Croydon Art Collection, Croydon Clocktower

double-shuttered sails, the old mill was sold for £1000 to Aaron Ashby of Warlingham. The so-called new mill was owned by the Byrons and leased by Alfred Gilbert, baker, but worked by John Tutt and later his father and brother. The old mill was refurbished by Thomas Rivers who re-cogged the brake wheel and renewed the tail post. There is no record of this mill after 1885. When the old mill was dismantled its oak centre post was used in the hall of Coulsdon Court. The new mill stopped work in 1912, and in October 1922 it was sold to William Wood, who demolished it about two years later.

The local **blacksmith** was in Coulsdon Road on the corner of what is now Waddington Avenue, hence Forge Avenue, and there was a small **brickworks** on the site of The Crossways, which was last used to make the bricks for Coulsdon Court in 1850.

The Forge at Old Coulsdon

Now a petrol station, at the corner of Waddington Avenue

1933

From a watercolour by Ethel Hall

Courtesy Croydon Art Collection, Croydon Clocktower

PUBLIC SERVICES AND INDUSTRY

At Smitham Bottom there was no industry until the early years of the 20th century. With the development of Coulsdon, Charles Wakeling started a blacksmith's in Chipstead Valley Road in 1915. He had been a blacksmith on the Webb Estate in Purley. He specialised in ornamental metalwork and garden gates. One of his grandsons, Brian Wakeling, while on active service in Suez in 1956 recognised some of the firm's work. The firm closed in 1992.

When the London Brighton & South Coast Railway built its new line – the Quarry Line – in 1899 it decided to make Coulsdon the terminus for suburban services. There was plenty of spoil excavated from the cuttings and tunnel at Merstham to provide foundations for carriage sidings and a locomotive depôt. The resulting works occupied the land between the main line and Brighton Road as far as Marlpit Lane and provided work for a considerable number of men. With the electrification of suburban railways the locomotive depôt closed, but the carriage works continued until the closure of Coulsdon North station in 1984. The site at Coulsdon North was then redeveloped as an industrial estate, and is now occupied by several companies specialising in freight transport (by road) and other warehousing activities.

During the early years of the 20th century **motor works and garages** began to appear. The first recorded are in Ward's Directory of 1922 when Haynes Brothers owned the Central Garage in Brighton Road between Victoria Road and Station Approach Road. Knight & Wheatley, Smitham Motor Garage, and Beart & Blackall were all occupying premises along Brighton Road. At this time many blacksmiths' premises were converting to, or being sold to garages, and this included the blacksmith's at Lacey Green shortly before World War II.

By the 1920s and 1930s, Coulsdon was beginning to assume its present appearance as a suburban area. Local businesses were builders and decorators, plumbers, printers, bootmakers, and of course garages. In the 1891 edition of Ward's Directory there are five commercial entries including Halls' Limeworks. In the 1922 edition this had grown to 17 including five garages.

SOURCES

Amberley Chalk Pits Museum

British Gas plc Archives

Bourne Society *Local History Records*

British Telecommunications Archives

Coulsdon & Purley Advertiser

Croydon Local Studies Library

DOBSON, C G (1951) *A Century and a Quarter.* Hall & Co Ltd, Croydon

FARRIES, K G & MASON, M T *Windmills of Surrey & Inner London.* Charles Skilton

Sutton & East Surrey Water plc

Ward's and Kelly's Directories

Coal Posts were erected at the boundaries of the Metropolitan Police district, at which point – about 20 miles from London – duties became payable on coal and wine coming into London. There are five posts in Coulsdon: Stites Hill Road, Coulsdon Road, Ditches Lane, Brighton Road and Hollymeoak Road. For further details see *Local History Records* 33 (1994).

Coulsdon C of E Primary School, Bradmore Green 1904
The school house is to the left

Photograph courtesy of Purley Library

Chapter 17

Schools & Colleges

by Margaret Davison & Jean Emery

The Education Acts of 1870 and 1880 formed the foundations of today's primary education. With these Acts schooling became compulsory and the State began to take responsibility for the education of its people. Prior to this date, it was mainly the Church that took the initiative in setting up schools and Coulsdon was no exception. The rector of St John's church, the Revd William Wood, had set up a school in a cottage by 1834 and was supporting it entirely, well before the 1870 Education Act. This cottage school, the forerunner of Coulsdon Church of England Primary School on Bradmore Green, would have been a dame school. Most villages had dame schools, usually run by an old lady who taught her charges to read, write and do simple sums. A small fee was often charged for this amenity. Fees for primary education continued to be paid until they were abolished in 1914.

COULSDON CHURCH OF ENGLAND PRIMARY SCHOOL *(now* Bradmore Green School), Bradmore Green

When the Bishop of Winchester asked the Rector of Coulsdon in 1788 how many schools there were in the Parish, the answer was 'None'. The first school associated with St John's church was established in 1834 in a small cottage by the rector the Revd William Wood, at his personal expense. In 1845 Squire Thomas Byron donated a parcel of land – the present site – and a small school building opened as the Coulsdon National School, in its turn replaced in 1888 by another larger school with a house for the master where the present playground is located. The school was the only one serving a wide area, and children from as far away as Hooley and Kenley walked there and back daily in every kind of weather. From 1912 Miss Churchill, the headmistress, lived in the schoolhouse until 1932, when she was still teaching 'with undiminished vigour and zeal'. There was an osier bed from which canes were cut to punish the fractious.

The school was typical of its time and right to the end in 1963 had the facility of outdoor lavatories for both boys and girls. As the number of pupils grew, additional temporary classrooms were added until in 1963 the old building was demolished and the present one built. Several more classrooms have been added in recent years.

BYRON INFANTS AND JUNIOR SCHOOLS, St David's, Stoneyfield Road

Byron School was opened in 1968. It was originally called Stoats Nest School but was renamed Byron School after the Byron family. From 1968 to 1977 it was a combined Infants and Junior school and in 1977 a separate Infants school building was opened.

CHIPSTEAD VALLEY SCHOOL, Chipstead Valley Road

This school has served the community since it opened as a Mixed Infants and Junior school in 1932, with seven classes and 246 children. The Secondary School opened in 1937 and closed in 1969, when the students were transferred to the extended Woodcote County Secondary School. The Junior School then moved into its former building.

Following the outbreak of war in 1939 the school delayed opening for the autumn term for six weeks, when a full roll of 383 children was recorded. On 11 July 1944 the school was badly damaged by a bomb. Fortunately there were no casualties and four children even returned for lessons in the afternoon. In 1945 peace was celebrated with a two-day holiday on 8 & 9 May. Another holiday shared with all schools was on 1 & 2 June 1953 for the Coronation of Queen Elizabeth II.

On 17 May 1974 the swimming pool was opened by the Mayor of Croydon, and in 1987 the school expanded to the present structure of three-form entry.

CLIFTON HOUSE SCHOOL, 77 Brighton Road

A preparatory day school for both girls and boys, which gave a good educational foundation up to the age of 10 or 11, run on modern lines under the tutelage of the Principals, Mrs and Miss De Ville. There was a large garden where tennis and hockey were played. Country dancing was also taught. The school appears to have been started around 1924 as a private venture by the De Villes and survived until at least 1959.

COULSDON HIGH SCHOOL (*formerly* Taunton Manor High School) Homefield Road

The school was built in 1964 and until 1971 as a county secondary school catered for 11-16 year old pupils. It then became a comprehensive school with an age range of 11-14, when the pupils went on to high schools, mostly to Purley Boys' and Purley Girls' then still in Old Coulsdon. The age range was extended to 16 in 1985. Another change took place in 1994 when it became a grant-maintained school managed by local governors directly responsible to the Secretary of State for Education.

**Coulsdon High
School in 1975**

*Photograph
courtesy of
Purley Library*

The school took its original name from the land it stands on. After the capture of Acre in 1191 during the Crusades led by Richard I, a priest named de Taunton established a small hospital to care for the wounded on land granted by the Abbot of Chertsey from within his manor of Coulsdon and this came to be called Taunton sub-manor. The original badge of Taunton Manor School made reference to this history by the inclusion of the Maltese cross used in the arms of the monastic Hospital of St Thomas of Acre. The school badge also made reference to the arms of Coulsdon & Purley Urban District Council with two sprigs of oak, and specifically to the hill on which Old Coulsdon stands by the inclusion of a green chevron depicting the hill and the adjoining Green Belt. The High School badge which has replaced it and which was designed by Lauren Step, a senior pupil, retains the Maltese cross.

DOWNLAND SCHOOL, Coulsdon Road

This was a private school opened in 1932 in her house, 'Pound Cottage', by Miss Doris Martin. There were about 50 children in three classes, girls aged 4-11 being prepared for the 11-plus examination for Purley Girls' School or entrance examinations to other private and public schools, and boys 4-7 in a kindergarten. The school was closed in 1962, though Miss Martin continued to live in 'Pound Cottage' until her death in 1993. HM the Queen, when still HRH Princess Elizabeth, once stopped and spoke to the children when on her way to Caterham Barracks as Colonel-in-Chief of the Grenadier Guards there. *(Photograph taken about 1942).*

FAIR DENE SCHOOL, 3 Reddown Road

The school was founded in 1911 as an independent public day school with 69 pupils, providing education for girls to the age of 11 and boys to 7. In 1941 it was bought by Theodora Turner and Helen Delmege, who transferred it to 60 Downs Road (now a nursing home and day centre). When it opened the school charged three guineas per term. In 1948 it moved to Pirbright Manor, Hog's Cross Lane, Chipstead, where boarding facilities were offered. It closed voluntarily in 1984.

KESTON INFANTS' AND JUNIOR SCHOOLS, Keston Avenue

Originally called Keston Avenue School, it was founded in 1937 and the present junior school building dates from then. A separate infants' school was built in the same grounds in 1959. During World War II, from September 1939 to January 1946, the school shared its buildings with Coulsdon C of E Primary School.

Like Taunton Manor School, Keston is built on the grounds of Taunton sub-manor and for this reason also uses the crusaders' Maltese cross on its badge.

PURLEY COUNTY SCHOOL FOR BOYS (*later* Coulsdon College), Placehouse Lane

The original school was opened in 1914 in the converted Commemoration Hall in Godstone Road, Purley, until recently occupied by Shaftesbury Independent School. On the first day there were only 48 boys but within the first year the numbers rose to 260.

With over 300 pupils, the school moved to a new building in Placehouse Lane, Old Coulsdon in 1933, when Alderman Chuter Ede, Chairman of Surrey County Council, handed over the school to the governing body whose chairman was F H B Ellis. It was a grammar school, taking boys from 11 to 18 until reorganisation of the education system in 1972 when it became a comprehensive school for boys aged 14-18.

The summer holidays of 1988 marked the start of a phased development, refurbishment and extension of the buildings, which continued until 1991. It was formally opened as Purley Sixth Form College by Sir William Clark MP in March 1992 and in April 1993 was renamed Coulsdon College.

Purley County School 2nd XV. 1943 - 44.

G. Robson,   D. J. Fawcett,   J. O. Elwood,   G. L. Benzon,   D. W. Walker,   D. E. Goodman,   W. D. Howson,   T. E. Couling

D. S. Clifford,   J. R. Buxton,   B. C. Davies,   J. C. Burt,   J. D. Scott,   T. F. Buxton,   D. Brown
(Captain)

On the occasion of Purley Grammar School for Girls Senior Speech Day, March 1958

Over the period 1914 to 1988 there were only five headmasters: 1914 – R B Wight; 1920 – B E Mitchell; 1945 – Dr H Birchall; 1966 – Acting Headmaster A Jewitt; and in 1969 D G S Akers. Among notable former pupils are the actors Peter Cushing and Alan Curtis, and the runner Gordon Pirie.

Despite its proximity to Kenley Aerodrome the school was not evacuated during World War II. No bombs damaged the school though a Hawker Hurricane fighter crashed on the playing fields.

PURLEY COUNTY SCHOOL FOR GIRLS (*later* Purley High School) Stoneyfield Rd

The Girls' Grammar School was founded in the former Commemoration Hall, Godstone Road, Purley, in 1933, the Boys' School having moved to Placehouse Lane. There were three classrooms, a hall, a laboratory and an art room, served by four staff and a headmistress – Miss J C Simpson – who presided until 1962. Starting with 26 girls, by 1935 the number had risen to 125.

Purley County School for Girls in the 1950s. Site sold for redevelopment in 1992

The move to the new building in Stoneyfield Road took place in January 1939. The school was officially opened by Sir Philip Henriques. 300 pupils attended, although the premises could accommodate 480. The large playing fields had hockey pitches, and tennis and netball courts, giving opportunities for games not available at Godstone Road.

On the outbreak of war in September 1939, opening for the autumn term was delayed until November while air-raid shelters were constructed. The coming of war meant that a large number of girls were taken away to be educated privately or transferred to schools closer to home, but others moving into the district kept up the numbers. In 1944, with the arrival of the V1 pilotless bombs, a party of girls was evacuated to Tyldesley, Lancashire, but the Stoneyfield Road premises remained in use. The end of the war saw 520 pupils on the roll, the maximum capacity of the school building.

It remained a grammar school, taking girls from 11 to 18, until the reorganization of the education system in 1972 when it became a comprehensive school – girls only – with an age range of 14-18. In 1988 it became part of Purley Sixth Form College, and once alterations at the former Boys' School in Placehouse Lane had been completed the Stoneyfield Road premises were closed. The site was sold for redevelopment in 1992.

ROSSLYN SCHOOL OF DANCE AND DRAMA, Reddown Road

Founded in 1947 by Mrs Cynthia Coatts, who also taught at Fair Dene school for many years, the school takes students of all ages, bringing them up to diploma level examinations at the Royal Academy of Dancing and the London Academy of Music and Dramatic Art.

ST AIDAN'S (ROMAN CATHOLIC) PRIMARY SCHOOL, Portnalls Road

The school was opened in 1976 on its present site across the road from its mother church. A number of additional temporary classrooms have been added since then, required to meet an increasing number of pupils. Mrs T M Hobbs has served as headmistress ever since the school was founded.

ST ANNE'S SCHOOL, The Drive

Founded in 1912, day boys from the age of 4 to 13 were provided with a thorough preparation for grammar and public schools and for the Royal Navy. The classes were small, and great importance was attached to the development of character and to high standards of manners and behaviour. The school later started to take boarders, who were in the care of the headmaster's wife, Mrs Leathley.

((Photograph taken c.1937 – Nigel Davison standing, Roger Davison to his right).

ST PETER'S SCHOOL FOR GIRLS, The Chase

With money provided by Mr Allen, the school was opened in 1925 at No. 28 The Chase with a dual headship – Mr Allen's daughter Ethel and her friend Miss Olive Gooch. It was extremely small until the adjacent plot was developed in about 1928, and by 1939 there were 108 pupils including five boys in the kindergarten class. Girls were taken from the age of five to 18.

Evacuated for a week during the Munich crisis of 1938, the school left Coulsdon again a year later at the outbreak of war, and some of the pupils went to Topsham in Devon with Miss Allen and Miss Gooch where they remained for the duration, while the remainder stayed in Coulsdon – effectively two St. Peters'.

In 1940 the school was purchased by Mrs G A Lord. The number of pupils remained quite low during the war years, but the school grew dramatically from the middle of the 1950s. No. 28 became part of the school, Mrs Lord moved to No. 34 and in 1957 No. 32 (The Cottage) became the 6th Form Centre. Mrs Lord remained headmistress until she was taken ill in 1973 and the school had to be closed somewhat abruptly in July of that year. There were then 288 pupils including two boys, together with 20 teachers.

SHERBORNE SCHOOL FOR GIRLS, The Grove

Opened in the 1920s by Miss Constance Horsey, the school fulfilled a preparatory function to qualify pupils for public schools. With small classes and fully-qualified teachers, a thorough grounding through modern methods covered academic subjects as well as needlework, handwork and physical education. Music too was taught, pupils being prepared for the Associated Board of Music examinations.

SMITHAM SCHOOL, Portnalls Road

With the construction of Cane Hill Asylum in 1883, with a staff of 500 and additional railway workers, a second school in addition to Bradmore Green was needed to accommodate the increasing number of children.

The school was opened on a temporary basis in the corrugated iron mission hall in Brighton Road, where the Comrades Club is now. It was known as the Cane Hill C of E Mission School. The morning it opened in November 1886, 46 children attended, but 48 came that afternoon. Most had never been to school before and there were only four who could read even short words and 10 who knew their alphabet. Writing and counting were at the same backward state. The schoolmistress Miss Fanny M Webb had just one monitoress to assist her to arrange regular attendance of the pupils, whose ages ranged up to eight years old. Thereafter they went to Bradmore Green, which had new premises built in 1888.

Class of Smitham Infants' School 1924-25

(Back row): **Charlie Phillips, Gwen Dellar, Margaret Jones, Lucy Brown, Phyllis Hooker, Ted Purver, Peter Barton**

(Front row): **Eileen Nestor, Margaret Wheeler, Jean Heron, Peggy Izzard, Fred Matthews, Jackie Brown**

Photograph courtesy of Purley Library

The 'school pence' (parents paid a small weekly fee for their children's attendance) were collected and entered in a logbook, together with the average attendance, which appears to have been about 50 children.

Squire Edmund Byron donated a triangular plot of land in 1892 on the corner of Chipstead Valley Road and Woodcote Grove Road (then called Smitham Bottom Lane) for a new school, originally conceived as a separate school to the mission hall. It was to be called Smitham Bottom Infants' School, under its own management and staff. However it was soon decided to treat the new school as a continuation of the old one. Opened in 1893, it suffered from the inadequacies of the building itself and of its teaching staff.

Following the 1902 Education Act the school became the responsibility of the Surrey Education Committee and in 1905, 57 children were transferred to the temporary buildings of the Coulsdon & Purley Smitham Bottom Council Mixed School and numbers attending increased considerably. In May 1908 staff and pupils moved into the permanent building fronting on to Chipstead Valley Road. Extra accommodation was completed for the infants and the old 1905 iron premises taken down.

In 1932 the Chipstead Valley Road School opened and some of the juniors were transferred there, leaving Smitham as the Coulsdon & Purley Smitham Bottom Junior Mixed & Infants' Combined School under the headship of W Scott. The school was transferred to Chipstead Valley School in September 1939 for five months while air-raid shelters were built on the Smitham site.

In 1956 the Primary School, comprising eight junior classes and four infant classes, took over the Secondary School premises vacated when the older children transferred to the recently-built Woodcote School in Meadow Rise.

On the amalgamation of Coulsdon & Purley UDC with the Borough of Croydon in 1965, the school was administered by the Borough Education Committee and was called Smitham Primary School.

The school moved to new premises in Portnalls Road in September 1991, opened by Roy Castle, and the old school was given over to adult education.

TOLDENE PRIMARY SCHOOL, Drive Road

Toldene School was opened in 1957 in response to the increasing numbers of children in Coulsdon. By that time all the primary schools were full, some children having to be taken by coach to Smitham School.

Toldene began life in three temporary huts, the permanent school being built around them. It closed in 1980 because of falling rolls in the Borough generally and the buildings were added to and adapted for use as a sheltered housing unit for elderly people.

WOODCOTE SCHOOLS, Meadow Rise

Woodcote School opened in 1954 as Smitham (Woodcote) County Primary School and became an infants-only school following the opening of the junior school in 1962. At first the junior school comprised one classroom, a hall and two huts, and could take only about 80 children. After the building was extended in 1968, the capacity increased to 400.

Woodcote High School opened in 1905 as Smitham Central & Junior School in temporary buildings adjacent to Smitham Bottom Infants' School in Chipstead Valley Road. Over the years the school changed its name several times, but always had 'Smitham' incorporated in it. The school moved from the site in Malcolm Road to Chipstead Valley School for a short time during World War II while air raid shelters were built, when classes were held in the afternoons only. In 1944 large numbers of pupils were evacuated, leaving three functioning classes in the school, but numbers quickly rose again.

On moving to its present site in Meadow Rise in 1956 it became Woodcote County Secondary School. In 1972 its age range was reduced from 11-16 to 11-14 when it became a comprehensive school known as Woodcote High School. Since 1985 it has again taken pupils from the age of 11 up to 16, but remains a comprehensive school.

ADULT EDUCATION

There is a very wide range of vocational and non-vocational education for adults in the Coulsdon area. The old Smitham School in Chipstead Valley Road has been converted into a Day and Evening Centre and many other schools are used in the evenings.

SOURCES

BECKLEY, Pauline – St Peter's School

Bradmore Green Library Local History Book.

BROADBENT, U & LATHAM, R (Eds) (1976) *Coulsdon – Downland Village*. The Bourne Society

BUTLER, Berry, for Fair Dene School and Rosslyn School of Dance & Drama

Chipstead Valley School prospectus

Coulsdon High School

Coulsdon & Purley Urban District Council Official Guides, 1929 & 1967

Dr R C W Cox, Croydon School Archives

Croydon Library *Local History Pack.*

GARRARD, David. Headmaster, Smitham School

Purley Library

THARBY, W G (1972) *The History of Coulsdon West.* Coulsdon West Residents' Association

The Bourne magazine of Purley High School for Boys

W H Cooper's Boot & Shoe Shop in Brighton Road
***c.*1905**

Chapter 18

Shops

by Ian Scales

Possibly by virtue of the way it developed during the late 19th and the first half of the 20th centuries, Coulsdon must boast more separate shopping parades than most communities of its size. The hilly nature of the ground allowed economic justification for them springing up wherever a new estate was built, saving the housewife's legs from too much walking.

When Smitham Bottom was bare save for Brighton Road and *The Red Lion*, prior to the building of the railway in the 1830s, most of the population lived on the hill, and here Squire Byron leased out a cottage in Coulsdon Road, now 'Cherry Tree Cottage', to be used as a general store and post office. It also eventually had a beer licence, granted in 1878 by the squire in his position as Justice of the Peace, with the express rule that no wines or spirits be sold. It must have been a welcoming beer house for the field workers after a hard day's ploughing. There would have been small reason for shops as we know them now, since the farms where everyone worked provided everything needed on a day-to-day basis; the villagers would have had little or no money available for general shopping and the gentry would have used Croydon for other needs.

Brighton Road, looking north from near Lion Green Road, *c.*1920

The nearest shop is Beart & Blackall Ltd, a garage

All this changed with the coming of the railways in the 1840s and later the opening of the Cane Hill Asylum in 1883. Suddenly there were several hundred wage-earners living in the district, all wanting food, clothing, shoes and other necessities, so the first shops opened along Brighton Road, Lion Green Road and Chipstead Valley Road. Other services were supplied by housewives, such as laundry, tailoring and the like, working from home and very much on a part-time basis. The local constable seems to have specialised in cobbling, a trade he continued when the Metropolitan Police took over responsibility for law and order.

When Cane Hill opened there was a much larger influx of workers, all requiring homes and shops within walking distance. A few were purpose-built from the beginning, such as the group of four next door to *The Red Lion*, built around the time of the Boer War — look at the gable shape to be reminded of South African architecture. Most of the many small shops of today still use what were once houses, suitably modified by covering the little front garden with a shop-front up to the edge of the pavement. This is particularly noticeable with the shops facing the library on Brighton Road, where a few are still residences, set back from the road.

The coming of a reliable passenger rail service to London, following the opening of what is now Coulsdon South Station in 1889, resulted in the development of Fairdene, Downs and Reddown Roads at the turn of the century, together with the beginnings of development to the west. City gentlemen had money to spend, so that by 1903 there were 24 commercial establishments listed, mainly around Lion Green triangle, but also along Brighton Road opposite and beside *The Red Lion*—

Adkins, A	Bootmaker	Hawkins, T	Butcher
Almond, E	Bootmaker	*Herron, J	Sweep
*Angell, A	Baker & Confectioner	*Hill, T	Butcher
Ayles, T	Dairyman	Hooker, H	Insurance Agent
Bolton, E	Dairyman	Huggett, A	Bootmaker
*Carey, J	Grocer & Post Office	*Lambirth, W	General Stores
*Coppard, D	Temperance Hotel	Leisten, G	Hairdresser
*Eade, W	Tobacconist & Confectioner	Scoble & Co	Estate Agents
*Ebbutt, T	Undertaker	Spinner, H	Fruiterer
*Florence, J	Draper & Milliner	Trish, T	Contractor
Gillham, H	Ironmonger	Trish, T	General Store
Hawkins, M	General Shop	Wheeler, R	Carman

(*Located on Lion Green)

The specialised shops reflect the requirements then of the villagers, such as the need for three bootmakers, a tobacconist, a fruiterer as well as a grocer, a sweep and a carman. More shops were added in the 1920s to the north of the Smitham railway bridge, first on the west side of Brighton Road, then more with the construction of The Broadway on the east side facing The Avenue. This block was built around 1926, though before it was finished the builders went bankrupt, evident to this day from the roof line which was added hastily, causing extensive flood damage from rain after the flats and shops were occupied.

Aerial photograph of Smitham Bottom with *The Red Lion* left foreground and Brighton Road running from left to right.

1925

Photograph by Surrey Flying Services

Courtesy of Purley Library

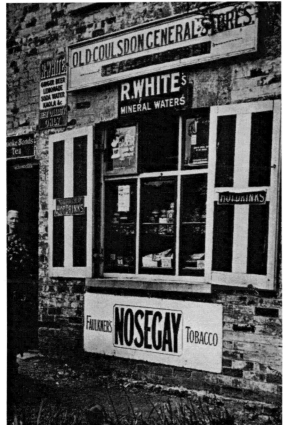

(Above): Brighton Road
looking north in the 1930s

(Left): Mrs Holland's
General Stores in Old
Coulsdon in 1932

It is now Cherry Tree
Cottage

*Courtesy of Croydon Local
Studies Library*

All were small shops, probably privately owned. Sainsbury's was the first of the multiples to arrive in 1912, next door to Barclays Bank – which building it owned – where Boots the chemist is now. Another multiple dating from World War II was MacFisheries, opposite *The Red Lion*, as was Liptons, where Lorimer's shop is now. Tesco came in the 1960s, building the large block next door to the Comrades Club, but only lasted a few years. Today most of the shopping done in Coulsdon is in Waitrose, on the corner of Malcolm Road for the past 30 years.

By 1939, the shops' and residents' list had expanded to include—

Lion Green Road, from Chipstead Valley Road towards Brighton Road—
Laurel Cottage and Cane Hill Cottages Nos 1 - 20 (including a local Policeman at No. 17).

Brighton Road, from the junction with Chipstead Valley Road—

150	National Provincial Bank		200	Gibbs, A	
152a	Pink Bros,	Radio Engineers	202	Carter, J	
152	Saunder & Co	Cycle Agents	204	Starling	
154	Curtis, W	Bootmaker/Leatherseller	206	Tench, J	Snack Bar
156	Driscoll, J	Tailor	208	Lawrence, H	Fruiterer
158	Shortell, L	Watchmaker	210	Southwell, V	Electrical/Radio
160	Hearne & Sons	Butcher	212	Booker, F	
162	Doe, A.	Fishmonger/Poulterer	214	Grover, G	Corn merchants
164	Croll, J	Newsagent/Tobacconist	216	Burnett, A	Confectioner
166	Symes, A	Draper	218	Webb, W	Builder/decorator
168	World's Stores Ltd		220	Webb, W	
170	Saunders & Co	Pram Depot	222	Heller, H	Optician
172	Elliots	Bootmakers	224	Coulsdon Garages Ltd	
174	Hawkins, F	Outfitter/Hosier	226	Coulsdon Garages Ltd	
176	Evans, C		228	Hill, M	Ladies' Hairdressers
178	Gibbs, H		230	Bevan, H	Cycles/Motorcycles
180	Bennett, E		232	Lesame,	Photographer
182	Dove, A		234	Scotchburn-Snell, P	
184	Cook, M Hairdresser (also Empress Laundry)		236	Webber & Harrison Ltd Furniture	

Chipstead Valley Road, from junction with Brighton Road—

1	Saunders & Co	Cycles/Sports/Toys	29	Lemmy, H	Fishmonger/Poulterer
3	Dorothy	Ladies Hairdressers	31	Maison Raphael	Hairdresser
5	Batty, E	Cabinet Maker	33	Coulsdon/Chipstead Laundry	
7	Shortell	Gents' Hairdressers	35	The Vic Wireless Stores	
11	Stanbridge	Hosier	37	" "	
13	"	"	39	" "	
15	Steward, F	Boot Stores	41	Wheeler, R	
17	Phoenix Cafe		43	Pollard, W	
19	Atkins & Co	House Agent	45	Lloyd, J	Valley Stores
	(also Coulsdon Printing Works)		47	Mervyn Coal Co	
21	Askew's Stores		49	Carder, A.	Butcher
23	Cook, E	Photographer	51	Thomson, H	Bootmaker
25	James, R	Radio/Electrical	53	Woollven, J	Confectioner
27	Downing, J	Confectioner/Tobacco	55	Eagle, A	Fruiterer/Florist

SHOPS

Of all the shops listed in 1939, only one remained under the same ownership until 2000 – Southwell's electrical shop – and now even this one has closed. Others have retained the same trading name, e.g. F W Woolworth & Co, Marsh's and The Downside Pharmacy, but are under different ownership.

For all the national competition, Coulsdon still boasts around a hundred small shops on and around Brighton Road. The trend in recent years is reflected in the number of eating places – impossible to count exactly since they come and go so often – and the outlets for alcohol. 50 years ago there was *The Red Lion* and its associated off-licence; now there must be a dozen bars and licensed restaurants as well as several off-licence shops.

Tudor Parade, Old Coulsdon, in the 1950s

Taaunton Lane shops in the late 1930s

Evidence of further changes in needs can be seen nearly 30 years later, when by 1965 there were three wet-fish shops, three or four butchers, three bakers, four ladies' dress shops plus a milliner, and three men's outfitters.

What of the smaller shopping parades? Chipstead Valley Road was developed nearly as far as Rickman Hill by 1905, with a further burst of development in the mid-1920s, and it was not long before there was a set of shops at the bottom of Rickman Hill.

Lacey Green Shopping Parade 1999
Photograph courtesy of Roger King

The next major change to Coulsdon was the sale of the Coulsdon Manor lands in Old Coulsdon and Coulsdon East for housing development in the 1920s, though a smaller development occurred immediately after World War I with the building of Stoats Nest Village, and the first 'local' shops being built to serve a community separated by half a mile from the centre in Smitham Bottom.

With the commencement of the 'Tudor Village' around St John's Church in Old Coulsdon early in the 1930s, the next parade of shops was built, comprising a 'complete set' to satisfy local needs – The Old Coulsdon Café on the corner of Placehouse Lane was the first in 1933, jointly owned by Henry and Alice Oliver. They provided not only a greengrocer's shop and home baking by Mrs Oliver, but upstairs was the café or tea room which acted as a meeting-place for local clubs, and which was also popular for wedding receptions after the ceremony in St John's Church. During World War II the law insisted that all signposts and other clues to location be removed or painted out, so 'for the duration' The Old Coulsdon Café proclaimed itself as 'The Old Café'. The post office next door combined its trade with a haberdasher's shop. Next to them the essential newsagent's shop also sold confectionery and tobacco. An ironmonger and an off-licence completed the first block. The second half of the parade comprised a butcher, a hairdresser, an estate agent, a chemist, a bakery and finally Cullen's, one branch of many owned by that company, which were general food shops. There are still nine shops plying the same trades to this day; only an ironmonger is absent from the list.

SHOPS

The development of Old Coulsdon in the 1930s added more parades – at Lacey Green near the old forge, and another close by in Taunton Lane which served the development around The Glade, each comprising more-or-less a complete set.

Another parade on the Clock House Estate (The Mount) to the west was built in the 1950s, essential if the residents there were to avoid a long trek to Smitham Bottom, since the bus service was until recently very uncertain.

**Brighton Road, looking north from the junction with
Chipstead Valley Road 1999**

Photograph courtesy of Roger King

There have been many changes in trade and style over the past century and there will be many more in the future. As industry in Coulsdon changes, so will the shops, but it is beyond imagination, despite occasional scares, that they will not survive in some form in the future.

SOURCES

Barclays Bank plc

Coulsdon Library

Pam Dutnell

Bob Johnson

Gwen Yarham

Ye Olde Foxe (Now *The Fox*) in the 1930s. The chestnut tree,
with its shady seating, has long since gone

Coppard's Temperance Hotel at Old Man's Corner at the junction
of Lion Green Road and Brighton Road. *c.*1910

Courtesy of Croydon Local Studies Library

Chapter 19

Leisure Activities

by Gwyneth Fookes

Some leisure activities have changed little over time – many people still enjoy spending time at their local hostelry as they have done through the centuries. People still enjoy walking, riding, racing and knocking a ball about, but these activities have become more formal during the latter years of the 20th and into the 21st century. Other organisations have arisen and thrive, such as sports clubs in a wider sense, social clubs and those with charitable aims. Coulsdon has a wide complement of activities.

Public houses occurring in old records include *The Red Lion* and *The Fox* with more recent public houses *The Tudor Rose, The Wattenden Arms,* and *The Jack & Jill,* opening to meet the needs of the expanding population. *The Red Lion* is shown but not named on John Seller's map of 1680, and parts of the original building and stables existed until rebuilding in 1928. A local inn named *The Fox* has been on Coulsdon Common for at least 200 years. Before the present road to Caterham was built in 1856 it faced the old road to the west side of the present building. The *Pig & Whistle* once occupied the thatched cottage in Old Lodge Lane. At the beginning of the 20th century Coppard's Temperance Hotel at the corner of Lion Green Road was very popular with cycling club enthusiasts after they had been conducting trials up the deeply-rutted Marlpit Lane.

Physically Energetic Pursuits

Racing & Rallying – John Seller's 1680 map shows Brighton Road as 'horse race' and 'unfenced'. The road from London to Brighton was then and still is a popular one for race challenges, its 50 mile length proving to be an appropriate length. To many the Veteran Car Rally is the most familiar and crowds still turn out early on the first Sunday in November to cheer the competitors.

London to Brighton Walking Race passing Woodplace Lane, 1903

Photograph by Miss E Tucker

Courtesy of Purley Library

Cricket in the parish dates to at least 1731, and a match played in 1762 gave the Old Coulsdon Cricket Club an excuse to claim a bicentenary in 1962. The club has since left its ground in Grange Park to play at the Ring, Redhill and become Redhill & Old Coulsdon CC. There are records of important early matches played on Lion Green opposite *The Red Lion* and Cane Hill Asylum could boast a strong team for many years from the 1880s. The East Coulsdon Residents' Association set up East Coulsdon CC in Marlpit Lane in 1947 and in 1974 this club merged with Chipstead CC to form the present Chipstead & Coulsdon CC.

The **Old Purleians Rugby Football Club** was started in 1927 – by former pupils of Purley County Grammar School – when matches were played at Grange Park. A team photograph of that year includes the actor Peter Cushing. The team changed in a wooden hut in the garden of the cottage – which was then the village shop – just outside the churchyard. Occasional teams were fielded during the war and the official opening of the clubhouse and ground at Parson's Pightle took place on 22 April 1961. In recent years the club became open to all players, when it became Purley RFC. A merger with the old boys of John Fisher School is responsible for the present name of Purley-John Fisher RFC.

The Rugby Football Club clubhouse, photographed in 1961.

Photograph courtesy of Purley Library.

The **Coulsdon Football Club** was formed in 1923 and played in the Premier Division of the Croydon Mid-week League. A very successful side, in 1934-35 it won the Croydon League, Division I Cup and the following season, the East Surrey Hospital Cup. A photo of the team appeared on an Ardath cigarette card.

The senior Association Football club in Coulsdon is **Woodland Albion F C**, which plays at Rickman Hill Recreation Ground. The club started in 1947 with a series of friendly matches and joined the Redhill & District League the following year. It still competes in that league and a special match was played in 1997 to mark the club's 50th anniversary and the involvement of manager John Green for its entirety.

On 9 June 1788 a **bare-knuckle prize fight** took place near *The Red Lion* between Gentleman Jackson and William Fewtrell. The Prince of Wales watched. Another major fight took place there on 14 May 1792 before 10,000 spectators.

The **Old Surrey Hounds** were housed at Garston Hall near *The Wattenden Arms* in the 19th century. Tom Hills, said to be 'the best huntsman who ever lived', became Huntsman at the age of 20 in 1816 and held the post

565 Searchlight Battery, Royal Artillery, T.A. *c.*1947 **Photograph courtesy of Jean Emery**

Coulsdon Sports & Social Club presentation after a sponsored swim for charity. Left end poolside – Geoff Tomlinson, right end – Bill Aldridge
1992

until 1860. The hunt uniform then was a green coat and a 'beaver' hat. The **Surrey Staghounds** also ranged throughout the district – in 1903 they had to suspend hunting because of the heavy ground.

Nowadays the **Hash House Harriers**, which began on 18 November 1984 run/jog/stumble across the Downs in pursuit of little piles of sawdust dropped the day before at strategic intervals. The 14 original enthusiasts have never looked back, and the Hash continues vigorously to this day. One of the highpoints was their organisation of an April 1986 Sport-Aid run from Coulsdon Court. Over 500 ran the course they laid, in a carnival atmosphere, and they raised more than £71,000 for overseas aid.

The **South London Harriers** train in Coulsdon and Crystal Palace and hold competitions and social events.

Walker Miles (Edmund Seyfang Taylor), founder of the **Ramblers' Association**, was one of the first people to encourage walkers to get off the beaten track to enjoy the countryside and one of his *Field Path Rambles* published in 1904 gives details of a ramble from Stoats Nest Station to Woodmansterne and Chipstead.

Expansive **Coulsdon Common, Kenley Common, Farthing Downs and Riddlesdown** were formally dedicated as open spaces in perpetuity in 1883 and provide 21st century residents with plentiful walking space within the built-up areas. They are owned and managed by the Corporation of London. **Happy Valley** belonging to the London Borough of Croydon connecting Farthing Downs and Coulsdon Common completes the very large and environmentally attractive green tract of countryside.

Old Coulsdon Bowling Club – has some of the finest bowling greens in Surrey. It is tucked away at 81 Coulsdon Road and there is a handsome clubhouse with bar facilities, together with three indoor rinks for winter bowling. Outdoors there are two greens for summer play, which are very well used. The club has about 280 members, 170 men and 110 ladies and is thriving. Ernie Lake represented England many times in the 1950s and 1960s and many others have represented the county. The club was formed in 1936, when the late Arthur Markwick, a well-known butcher, provided most of the funds to purchase the two bowling greens, the original clubhouse and accommodation for a steward.

Coulsdon Court Golf Course – When the Byron estate was sold in 1922, the parkland became a golf course designed by Leslie Cotton, Henry Cotton's brother, who was appointed the club professional. Before World War II it was a private club owned by its members, but the government requisitioned it, using the house as a mess for servicemen and women. After the war the Coulsdon & Purley UDC took it back and the course was repaired, filling bomb craters as well as relaying the turf where there had been fields growing cereals. Coulsdon Court Golf Club resumed as a public amenity, open to anyone to play. The **Artisans' Golf Club** started in 1946, the **Ladies' Golf Club** in 1947 and the **Veterans' Golf Club** in 1949.

To the north of the parish **Woodcote Park Golf Club** is proud of Zane Scotland, the youngest player in the British Open in 1999.

Coulsdon Methodist Badminton Club – The club was founded in 1950 and it has a membership of 15-18 ladies and gentlemen. They play league and friendly matches and have a number of social events throughout the season. They meet at the Coulsdon Methodist church hall, but are not affiliated to the church.

Sports & Social Club – In 1974 the swimming pool at Chipstead Valley Primary School was completed after years of the children bringing sixpences to school each week. The teachers started the children's lessons and they would go home and ask mum or dad to take them swimming, so Bill Aldridge and Geoff Tomlinson offered their services to teach adult beginners to swim. They have been doing this for 25 years, providing the teaching on a voluntary basis, only charging to cover pool time. In 1992 a sponsored swim raised £750.

Territorial Army – The Marlpit Lane drill hall houses the local Territorial and Cadet units, and there are various lecture rooms and offices, with a miniature rifle range running the length of the building affording practice with .22 calibre rifles. The drill hall was home to 'R' Battery 565 Light Anti-aircraft Regiment TA, which until 1955 also incorporated a searchlight detachment 'manned' by women of the ATS. The speed of modern aircraft saw the demise of the LAA units in 1961 and as the guns fell silent the Paschal Lamb found itself presiding over the Royal Corps of Signals in the form of Princess Louise's Kensington Regiment. Local organisations use the hall for dances, shows and other activities.

Social Activities

The **Coulsdon Forum** 'of voluntary bodies working together for a better Coulsdon' was formed in 1980 to co-ordinate the work of those organisations which had a community dimension to their activities. In the early days there were eight member bodies, mainly residents' associations and churches; there are now 11 members. The inclusion of the Chamber of Commerce and the Women's Institute has broadened the representation of the community. It has become in effect a civic society interested primarily in welfare and environmental matters, endeavouring in the absence of a statutory parish council to be a think-tank and a voice for Coulsdon.

The **Working Men's Club** was established in November 1903, with a subscription of 8d a month. It met then at St Andrew's Mission Hall and was at the time asking in the local paper for equipment such as billiard tables. The workmen's concert advertised on 13 February 1904 was a typical event. A newspaper reference to the **Hope of Coulsdon Lodge** also meeting at St Andrew's Mission Hall in 1903 relates to the temperance movement.

**Coulsdon Working Mens' Club, founded 1903 next to Coppard's Temperance Hotel
The site was later occupied by Beart & Blackall's garage.**

Victoria Club – The club in Victoria Road dates from the 1920s and was originally built to house the Coulsdon Working Men's Club. There was a Railwaymen's Club on Station Approach Road, where Plumb Center (M A Ray's) is now and the Victoria Road club was built behind it.

Masonic Lodges – By their nature Masonic Lodges cannot often be geographically specific, but Coulsdon can claim to be one such. Confusingly named Woodcote Lodge, No 4891 in the United Grand Lodge of England (there was already a Coulsdon Lodge, though with few local connections), it was consecrated on 14 February 1927. All the 15 founders were professionals, such as doctors, dentists, a lawyer and businessmen – mostly shopkeepers – living or working in Coulsdon. It now meets in the Croydon Masonic Hall in Oakfield Road.

Rotary Club of Coulsdon – The Club was formed in 1928 with 15 – soon to become 24 – members, with the first president being Revd S W G Frost. Apart from a period in the 1970s when it met at Coulsdon Court, it has met for lunch at *The Red Lion*. During World War II the club adopted 615 Squadron, RAF Kenley, and also two minesweepers *Eileen Emma* and *Lord Inchcape* – both sadly were sunk. In 1940 rotarian Dr Cromie was killed on duty during a daylight raid on Kenley airfield. From 1976, in conjunction with the Variety Club of Great Britain, Coulsdon Rotary has run the Starlight Night at Fairfield Halls, which has raised £23,000 over the years. In 1978 it was attended by Princess Anne in aid of the Diamond Riding Stables. In 1983 the **Rotary Club of Coulsdon Manor** was formed, dining weekly at Coulsdon Manor Hotel. Its main fund-raising event is the Old Coulsdon Summer Fair held in Grange Park. In 1933 The **Inner Wheel Club** was formed for Rotarians' wives and it has subsequently given wonderful service both on its own account, and in support of Rotary.

Coulsdon & Purley Debating Society – One of only three debating societies in south east England. Started for men only; from before World War I there had been a move to include women as members, but it was 1981 before they were allowed. Now they form the majority of members and take a full part in the fortnightly debates. It meets in the Day Centre at Old Coulsdon. Well over 1,000 debates have taken place over 90 years; in many instances the decisions made have been adopted shortly afterwards by national government, though a direct link is tenuous!

Old Coulsdon Women's Institute – In October 1932 Lady Goodenough held the first meeting of the Institute. A room in the stable block at Parson's Pightle became its meeting place on the second Tuesday of the month. In the early 1980s it moved to St John's Hall and now meets on the second Monday of the month in the Cameron Hall.

Old Coulsdon Women's Institute's display of dolls made and dressed to show passing fashions 1972

LEISURE ACTIVITIES

Old Coulsdon (Evening) Townswomen's Guild – Held its first meeting on 11 November 1960 in St John's Hall. There were 120 members and 23 on a waiting list. Meetings later moved to Purley High School for Girls and are currently held in the Cameron Hall, with a membership of 63 of whom six are proud to be founder members. They do not now have a waiting list but that was because the original Guild split and the **Old Coulsdon (Tudor) TWG** was formed.

National Women's Register, Coulsdon & Purley Branch – Initially founded to promote a friendly and stimulating environment away from household and family chores, following the amazing response to a letter printed in *The Guardian* in the late 1960s. It was originally called 'the National Housewives' Register' and is a lively minded group of women who meet fortnightly at each other's homes. They discuss many issues including film, book and poetry reviews and current affairs.

Coulsdon Probus Club – Was formed on 4 April 1968 at a lunch meeting at *The Red Lion,* making it the second oldest Probus in the world after Caterham where the movement started. Specially for retired PROfessional and BUSinessmen, it meets monthly for lunch. In early days meetings featured after-lunch music, songs and comedy turns, but more recently these have been replaced by a visiting speaker. Golf and bowls sections are active and visits to places of interest regularly take place. A collection at table has enabled Probus to support local charities to a considerable extent.

Old Coulsdon Centre for the Retired – After two years' raising money in the local area, the Centre was opened in June 1984 by Cllr Mrs Maureen Hordern, Mayor of Croydon. It is open five days a week to provide meals and social activities. During the evenings and weekends the centre is used by many local organisations. The comfort and pleasant surroundings make it very popular for special family occasions.

In 1986 Dame Thora Hird presented a minibus to the Old Coulsdon Centre for the Retired as part of a 'Songs of Praise' TV programme

The **Coulsdon Chess Fellowship** meets at 84-90 Chipstead Valley Road.

There are a number of active **residents' associations** covering the parish – The Old Coulsdon Residents' Association, the East Coulsdon Residents' Association and the West Coulsdon Residents' Association.

The Arts

Cinema – *The Palladium* opened in Malcolm Road on Easter Monday 1914 with 350 seats. It had cost £860 to build. It closed on 26 February 1915 but was functioning again in June 1919. It was renamed *The Plaza* and was open from at least January 1927-1929 and then was known as *The Bijou* until the 1930s. The building remains.

Coulsdon & Purley Festival of Music, Speech and Drama – The Festival was founded in 1944 by E Bluett and Mrs Garfield Howe and its first president was Sir George Dyson, principal of the Royal College of Music. The current president is Marian Wey. In 1953 two sisters entered the Festival, playing to great acclaim – they were Hilary and Jacqueline du Pre, at that time residents of Purley. The Festival continues to flourish, recently adding a new jazz section to the existing piano, instrumental, vocal and drama sections.

Old Coulsdon Camera Club – was founded in December 1944 and has met since 1992 in the Methodist Hall.

The 35 Club – This club originates from an air-raid warden post, post No.35, which operated during World War II in Chaldon Way. The post generated a tremendous spirit of comradeship and goodwill to the extent that on cessation of hostilities the volunteers determined to maintain contact and formed a club, originally for the people who served at post 35. It is an independent club, not associated with any religious or political organisation. It recently celebrated its 50th anniversary.

The Chandos Choir – The Chandos Choir with some 40 members meets at Coulsdon Methodist Church Hall and rehearses under Ian le Grice. It was founded in 1950 by Bernard Rawlings as the Coulsdon & District Choral Society, becoming Coulsdon & Purley Choral Society before its present name. It has sung in a number of prestigious venues with many well-known soloists and made a recording of *Olivet to Calvary*.

Coulsdon Floral Arrangement Group – The Group was formed in November 1957 by Helen Davison and a few other ladies in a front room. It has flourished and it now has 56 members. They meet at Cameron Hall. The club over the years has arranged flowers at Ham House, Loseley, Southwark Cathedral and many local events. It celebrated its 40th anniversary with a wonderful meal and entertainment. It enjoys a summer and Christmas party. It holds workshops learning techniques on flower arranging and members regularly attend demonstrations at other clubs and venues.

Old Coulsdon Art Society – The Society was formed in 1962 by Mary Everitt and its function is to enable local amateur artists to practise and improve their skills in friendly company. Membership permits participation in the annual art exhibition organised each November, usually in the Arnhem Gallery in Fairfield Halls.

The Downland Chorale – Having started as 'Singing for Pleasure' under Gordon Bull, the choir developed under the title 'The Purley Philharmonic Society' with Paul Burnett. In 1989 Nicholas Houghton became director and when the choir moved from the Purley United Reformed Church to Coulsdon, it took its present name. Each year the Chorale presents four concerts which include *A Christmas Cracker* and an all-day workshop.

The OCRA Theatre Club – The club, which is a sub-section of the Old Coulsdon Residents' Association is in its 10th year organising five trips a year to theatres and concerts with the essential ingredient of travelling together by coach.

The Original Polygon Jazzband – Formed in 1984 by jazz musicians led on trumpet by Ken Coulbeck. It is a seven piece band with two vocalists – Audrey Stokes and Bev Steele. It is invited to play at jazz festivals, local carnivals, school and village fetes. It has been engaged for wedding celebrations and by clubs, pubs, on a riverboat for charity, and even in Hampton Court Palace.

Young People

Scouts – The Purley, Coulsdon & District B-P Scout Troop was formed in the first year of the Scout Movement, with Frank H Beckett as scoutmaster. He was killed during World War I. It met in a barn at Stoats Nest Farm. The scouts were not far away on 29 January 1910 when a train was derailed at Stoats Nest and they were soon on the scene and actively helped wherever they could. In the incident six passengers and one bystander died and 42 others were injured. For its fine example the Troop was awarded the Scout Medal of Merit, probably the first time an entire troop was so honoured by the Chief Scout.

Coulsdon Cub Scouts, then called Wolf Cubs, were first formed in Coulsdon in 1915 and the senior Scouts, then Rover Scouts, were formed in 1918. There are a number of active units in Coulsdon.

Guides – The Girl Guide movement was officially recognised in 1910, and the 1st Coulsdon Guide Company was registered in January 1922, meeting in Chipstead Valley Road The 3rd Coulsdon Guides opened in 1924 and the Brownies in 1927, meeting at the Methodist Church. Most of the churches in Couldson have had Guide companies and Brownie packs, formed prior to World War II, suspended during the war and since re-formed.

Coulsdon & District Guide Parade, Coulsdon Methodist Church, 18 July 1954

Photograph courtesy of Purley Library

In Old Coulsdon the first company to be registered was 2nd Coulsdon Guides on 24 November 1923. They met at Bradmore Green School and the original Guider was Miss Anne Goodenough, daughter of Admiral and Lady Goodenough. Lady Goodenough was Division Commissioner at the time. A Guide Rally, which the Chief Guide, Olave Lady Baden-Powell attended was held at Parson's Pightle in 1951. TV weather forecaster Helen Young was a guide in the 11th Coulsdon Guides.

There are now five Brownie Packs, five Guide Companies, a Ranger Unit and Trefoil Guild in Coulsdon and one Rainbow unit, five Brownie Packs, three Guide Companies and a Trefoil Guild in Old Coulsdon.

Coulsdon Youth Club & Social Centre in Chipstead Valley Road organises many activities, outings and fun nights.

There have almost certainly been a number of clubs, associations and activities not recorded in these pages; some no doubt because of unfortunate omission and others because no precise dates or other information was available to us.

SOURCES

BROADBENT, U & LATHAM R (Eds) (1976) *Coulsdon – Downland Village.* The Bourne Society

THARBY, W G (1972) *The History of Coulsdon West,* Coulsdon West Residents' Association Publication.

OCRA INSIGHT (1992). *The History of the Old Coulsdon Residents Association 1936-92*

Bourne Society *Local History Records*

Local residents

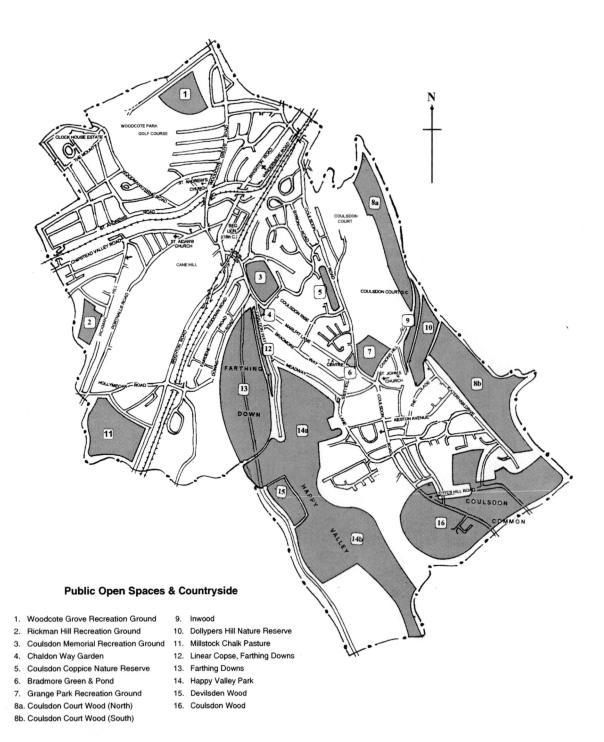

Public Open Spaces & Countryside

1. Woodcote Grove Recreation Ground
2. Rickman Hill Recreation Ground
3. Coulsdon Memorial Recreation Ground
4. Chaldon Way Garden
5. Coulsdon Coppice Nature Reserve
6. Bradmore Green & Pond
7. Grange Park Recreation Ground
8a. Coulsdon Court Wood (North)
8b. Coulsdon Court Wood (South)

9. Inwood
10. Dollypers Hill Nature Reserve
11. Millstock Chalk Pasture
12. Linear Copse, Farthing Downs
13. Farthing Downs
14. Happy Valley Park
15. Devilsden Wood
16. Coulsdon Wood

Chapter 20

Open Spaces and Countryside

by Eric W Groves

As may be seen from the accompanying map, apart from the wedge of housing development that occurred on the higher ground of Old Coulsdon during the 1920s and 1930s, the greater area of residential coverage is that towards the north of the parish and is on the lower ground. In consequence most of the open spaces and countryside that have been saved from urbanisation are to the south.

It is fortunate that it is still possible to walk through such areas as Happy Valley and over parts of Coulsdon Common and feel that one is miles from human habitation and the noise of traffic. There follows a brief description of the open areas and their attributes. Whether they are being visited for sporting activity or for the simple enjoyment that the surroundings may engender, Coulsdon can satisfy whichever purpose the visitor may seek—

1. Woodcote Grove Recreation Ground   *10 Acres (4.05 Hectares)*

An open field bordered with planted trees where children of nearby families can safely play away from traffic and where owners can exercise their dogs. 30 years ago one could frequently see lapwings feeding amongst the grass early in the morning, but unfortunately these have long since left the area.

2. Rickman Hill Recreation Ground   16.5 Acres (6.68 Hectares)

Situated on the west side of Rickman Hill, the recreation ground is surrounded by woodland on two sides and on the roadside it is bordered by a row of mature pine and larch trees of considerable height, interspersed with young oaks. Four football pitches, a cricket pitch in summer, and a playground for children provide considerable attraction for adults and youngsters alike. There is an attractive small area of woodland in the north-east corner, called Mother Kitty's Shaw, sparkling with wood anemones in the spring.

3. Coulsdon Memorial Recreation Ground   10 Acres (4.05 Hectares)

First opened to the public in 1921 in memory of those who fell in World War I, the Memorial Recreation Ground is situated to the east of Marlpit Lane and has tennis courts, a bowling green, an area in summer for a cricket pitch and a children's playground. There is also a small car park and a café, open all the year round.

4. Chaldon Way Garden.   0.5 Acres (0.20 Hectares)

A small ornamental garden situated at the bottom of Marlpit Lane at its junction with Chaldon Way. Seats allow the public to sit and enjoy the beautiful flowers and shrubs maintained there during the summer, before attempting the climb of Marlpit Lane!

5. Coulsdon Coppice Nature Reserve.   7 Acres (2.80 Hectares)

When Coulsdon Woods was developed as a housing estate in the 1960s, a small area of woodland and grassland on sloping ground was saved. This area, known as Larkins Dean and Bleakfield Shaw, lies on the upper chalk with part on clay-with-flints. It is now preserved as a nature reserve open to the public and supported by London Wildlife Trust, which leases it from the London Borough of Croydon. Maintenance work is carried out by a

(Left): Steps leading out of Bleakfield Shaw, Coulsdon Coppice Nature Reserve in 2000

(Below): A path through young trees in Larkins Dean, Coulsdon Coppice Nature Reserve 1999

spirited party of volunteers. Bleakfield Shaw contains oak (both pedunculate and sessile), ash, holly, field maple, wild cherry, blackthorn, hawthorn and dogwood. Present on the ground in spring are dog's mercury, moschatel and wood spurge – a number of the trees and ground species indicate that the shaw is old established woodland. Woodpecker, tree creeper, jay, tawny owl and rook have been observed there, while foxes may occasionally be seen crossing the paths, even during day time. Butterflies that have been recorded in summer have included the orange tip, comma, peacock, gatekeeper and ringlet. A small colony of Roman snails is also present.

6.   Bradmore Green & Pond   4 Acres (1.60 hectares)

A small triangular plot of grassland, now part of a Conservation Area, which lies at the junction of Marlpit Lane and Coulsdon Road. It was formerly part of the Byron family estate until purchased in 1922 by Coulsdon & Purley UDC. The pond, one of the few remaining on the clay-with-flints uplands of Old Coulsdon, is on record as having been artificially created in 1836 on behalf of Mrs Matilda Crowe in memory of her husband – on the site of an earlier pond, since one is shown on earlier maps. The wall behind the pond was built in 1969, after the long hot summer of that year. The pond has become dry on several occasions since but was recently deepened; much silt was removed under the direction of the Old Coulsdon Residents' Association.

7.   Grange Park Recreation Ground.   11 Acres (4.45 Hectares)

Originally part of Byron's Coulsdon Court park, this tree-surrounded recreation area was purchased from Coulsdon Court Golf Club in 1929, mostly by Coulsdon & Purley UDC. It has football, rugby and cricket pitches, a children's playground and toilet facilities. A further facility was added in 1984 when the Old Coulsdon Centre for the Retired was opened there. Like Bradmore Green, with which it combines, it now forms part of a Conservation Area.

8   **Coulsdon Court Wood** **(North: 8a, South: 8b)**   Approx 220 Acres including
146 Acres of 18-hole golf course

The North Court Wood is a linear woodland area to the east of the golf course, situated on the clay-with-flints plateau 400-500 ft above sea level. The wooded belt drops away steeply down to the gardens at the backs of houses in Old Lodge Lane. This mixed oak woodland additionally contains beech, yew, holly and wild cherry and through it weaves a variety of pleasantly shaded paths.

**Coulsdon
Court Golf
Course
backing on to
Coulsdon
Court Wood
(north)**

2000

**Grange Park
Recreation
Ground in the
1930s**

**Note
Bradmore
Green School
and the
Round House**

*Photograph
courtesy of
Purley Library*

The South Court Wood is really an extension of the same woodland belt beyond Inwood and Dollypers Hill Nature reserve (considered under areas 9 and 10). It is situated on rising ground between Old Lodge Lane and Caterham Drive. Like the North Court Wood, its tree cover is also of mixed oak. In spring the ground is patched with wood anemones.

9. Inwood (also on record as Ninwood and Linne Wood) 5 acres (2.02 Hectares)

This ancient semi-natural woodland, the northern part of which is now included in Dollypers Hill Nature Reserve, forms a tongue of land extending from behind the houses of Canons Hill northwards towards Old Lodge Lane. That part of the east side of the Lane towards Wattenden School consists of ash and hazel remaining from Victorian times, when it was frequently coppiced for hurdle/fence making. In spring Inwood becomes carpeted in bluebells and wood anemones – a magnificent sight!

An 1890s scene in Inwood

The hurdle-fence maker and his assistants by their pile of cut hazel sticks ready to be split and woven into hurdle fences for the local sheep farmers

Photograph courtesy of Purley Library

10. Dollypers Hill Nature Reserve 30 Acres (12 Hectares)

This nature reserve – created in the 1980s – consists of mixed woodland, scrub and grassland (the latter in the valley bottom). It is managed by Surrey Wildlife Trust under licence from the Borough of Croydon. The woodland part is on the steep western side and this drops down through scrub to the valley at the northern end of Caterham Drive. During spring, primroses flower in the grass on the lower slopes and a variety of orchids (pyramidal, common spotted and occasional bee and fly orchids) may be seen. The northern part of the reserve includes part of Inwood.

11. Millstock chalk pasture 60 Acres (23.27 Hectares)

Millstock was purchased by Coulsdon & Purley UDC in 1939 as part of the Green Belt, with additional land purchased later. Entry to its three fields is from a bridle path running between houses on the west side of

Woodfield Hill. The fields, lying on the upper chalk, are at present leased to a local farmer for grazing. Along the east side, abutting the back gardens of houses in Woodfield Hill, is a narrow belt of scrub hedgerow consisting of whitebeam, blackthorn, hawthorn and some seedling sycamore. The fields themselves are important botanically as the unimproved chalk grassland contains an impressive list of species including wild basil, marjoram, hairy St John's wort, yellow wort, felwort and a colony of the rare eyebright *Euphrasia pseudokerneri.*

12.　　Linear Copse, Farthing Downs　　　　7.25 Acres (2.83 Hectares)

This belt of trees is an ancient hedgerow running southward from Marlpit Lane to Drive Road. It forms a boundary below Farthing Downs to the west and the back gardens of houses in Chaldon Way and the northern end of Happy Valley, ending at that part termed Seven Acre Common. Its constituent trees and shrubs include oak, ash, beech, yew, field maple, holly, hawthorn and wayfaring tree.

13.　　Farthing Downs　　　　　　　121 Acres (49 Hectares)

Farthing Downs.
Looking from the Folly towards Cane Hill　1999

In conjunction with Linear Copse, Happy Valley and Coulsdon Common, this downland combines to form one of the most important calcicolous habitats in the Borough of Croydon and indeed in South London. The flat-topped ridge of Farthing Downs, extending north to south, rises about 150m. above sea level and is covered mainly by chalk grassland with patches of encroaching scrub. In summer this grassland contains perennials such as wild carrot, wild parsnip, burnet saxifrage, small scabious and two national rarities – the round-headed rampion and the greater yellow rattle. Farthing Downs is owned by the City of London Corporation and in recent years a small herd of cattle has been put to graze the coarser grasses. The scrub itself is occasionally coppiced to ensure a mix of young as well as mature bushes to provide shelter for nesting birds. Birds seen most years on the Downs include warblers, yellowhammer, skylark and green woodpecker. Foxes and rabbits are frequent, while smaller mammals – voles and shrews – may occasionally make their runs amongst the grass roots. A number of chalkland snails are present, notable among which is the Roman snail, which may be seen particularly after rain.

From Farthing Downs, looking south-east into Happy Valley

Before 1960

Happy Valley in earlier days

Children amongst the stooks of corn

Photograph courtesy of Croydon Local Studies Library

Happy Valley in 2000

Now a haven for botanists and dog-walkers

Cowslips in the foreground

14.   Happy Valley   252 Acres (101.37 Hectares)

This area occupies the length of the valley from the southern end of Chaldon Way to the parish boundary with Chaldon. For the purposes of this account it can be considered in two parts – the northern end and the southern end (14a and 14b respectively on the map). The whole area is maintained by the Borough of Croydon which mows the lower grass slopes after most of the wild flowers have seeded. Various orchids may be seen in spring, including the twayblade, pyramidal, fragrant, common spotted and some bee and fly orchids. A colony of the unusual woolly thistle has maintained itself on the valley floor, its existence there having been known to botanists for a number of years. At the southern end, cowslips cover the eastern slopes during April and towards Ditches Lane are two large fields, which lie on clay-with-flints and which are a blaze of yellow buttercups. In summer bird life includes yellowhammer, greenfinch, linnet, pheasant, kestrel and tawny owl. Among the mammals fox, badger, stoat, weasel and various species of mice have been noted in the valley. Summertime brings out a wide variety of butterflies and moths, including the red admiral, peacock, small tortoiseshell, brimstone, meadow brown, speckled wood, common blue and the six-spot burnet moth.

15.   Devilsden Wood   *c.*37 Acres (*c.*15 Hectares)

Situated within the western slope of Happy Valley about midway between areas 14a and 14b, this wood rises up to meet Ditches Lane. Unlike the remainder of the valley, which lies on chalk, the wood is on clay-with-flints. The dominant tree is oak, with yew, ash and wild cherry as sub-dominants. In spring, extensive patches of ground are covered with bluebells, wood sorrel, wood anemone and many other species that need to flower early in the season before the shade in the woodland becomes too deep. The mammals and birds within the wood are similar to those in Happy Valley.

Devilsden Wood

**The main path
through the wood,
now part of the
London Loop
Long-Distance Path**

2000

16.   Coulsdon Common   127 Acres (51 Hectares)

The Common consists of three main pieces of land – (a) that which lies between Stites Hill Road and Coulsdon Road, together with the area about *The Fox*, bounded on the south by The Grove. Most of this is flat, lies on heavy clay-with-flints and is covered by either oak woodland or meadow; (b) Rydon's Wood and the wooded area south of Stites Hill Road. Here the vegetation cover is oak woodland mixed with ash and hazel, having ground flora of bluebell, bugle, violets and forget-me-not; (c) is of undulating ground where the bedrock chalk comes close to the surface below the clay, as it does towards Hayes Lane. Here the woodland is replaced by meadow and downland. On its east-facing slope and in the valley floor ox-eye daisy and buttercup take over in May and June. Birds seen about the woods include woodpeckers, tree-creepers, tawny owl and – in spring – the blackcap. Grey squirrels and foxes are numerous, and if you are up at dawn you may catch a glimpse of the shy roe deer. The Corporation of London, which owns and is responsible for maintenance of the Common, manages the grass areas in three ways: the footpath grass is regularly mown but the open meadow areas are harvested as a hay crop late in the season when the wild plants have seeded. Since 1990 a small herd of Sussex cattle, some Southdown sheep and a number of Jacob sheep have been introduced to keep the coarser grasses in check.

Horse-riding on Coulsdon Common.   2000

SOURCES

CLENET, D, BRITTEN, B, & GAME, M (1988) *Nature Conservation in Croydon* (Ecology Handbook No.9)
  London Ecology Unit

Croydon Library

DOUGLAS, ROY (*c.*1990) Coulsdon Coppice Nature Reserve Guide

JONES, A W (1961) The Vegetation of Devilsden Wood and nearby Downs. *London Naturalist*, **41**: 77-86

Croydon Local Studies Library

London Borough of Croydon, Parks & Recreation Department

OCRA Insight: The History of the Old Coulsdon Residents' Association 1936 -1992

The History of Old Coulsdon (Local History Pack) Croydon Public Libraries

The Official Guide to Kent & Surrey Commons. City of London Corporation, 1992

WINTERMAN, M A (1988) *Croydon's Parks: an illustrated History.* Parks & Recreation Dept, London
  Borough of Croydon

Chapter 21

Personalities

by all contributors

D G S Akers MA (Oxon) – Headmaster of Purley County Grammar School for Boys (1969-1988). *See also* **Bertram E Mitchell**.

Mabel Lucy Attwell – lived at 'Fairdene', now 51 Fairdene Road, from 1920 - *c*.1930. She had married Harold C Earnshaw and moved from Dulwich to Coulsdon, living at first in a detached cottage-style house in Downs Road before moving to 'Fairdene'. It was while living in Coulsdon that she made her name writing children's books and designing postcards which featured her famous chubby children, 'Boo-Boos' drawings and plump puppies, published by Valentine & Sons. In about 1930 Mabel and her husband moved to East Sussex and eventually to Cornwall, where she died in 1964 in her 85th year.

Charles Babington – lived at The Grange for 14 years until 1914. He was a director of Watney's Brewery; he identified himself with local affairs and won the warm regard of all. His children were educated at Bradmore Green School and one was killed in the war. Mr Babington was treasurer of the school, a churchwarden and a vice-president of the local cricket club and Conservative Association.

D G S Akers, MA (Oxon)

Harry Borrodaile (born 1801) – was a resident at Coulsdon Court (now The Grange) soon after it ceased to be a farm in 1828, and appeared in the 1851 census with his wife Alexandrina and four children. He retired from the East India Company.

Una F D R Broadbent M A (Oxon) (1900-1984) – will be remembered as the author of *A Short History of Coulsdon* (1970) and as joint editor of *Coulsdon – Downland Village* (1976). Although born in Newcastle, her childhood summers were spent locally. She first stayed in Downs Road in 1906 – her home until she died. She wrote and broadcast for the B B C and taught for 24 years at Commonweal School, Purley. The Bourne Society's Bulletin was edited by her from 1965 until 1979 and she contributed several articles to *Local History Records* including her childhood reminiscences in Volume 3.

Baron Broadbridge of Brighton – George Thomas Broadbridge (1869-1952) was a self-made man with an exceptionally successful business career, a worker and supporter of many charities, active in public life, locally and nationally. He lived in Purley for nearly 30 years. As a member of Coulsdon & Purley District Council in 1928 he obtained Grange Park as a public open space. He was knighted in 1929 and eventually became Lord Mayor of the City of London in 1936. In 1938 he entered Parliament as Conservative member for the City of London and remained an MP until 1945, when he was created Baron Broadbridge of Brighton.

Byrons – They were the only Squires to live in the manor – see Chapter 7.

Nicholas Carew – in 1537 became Lord of the Manor of Coulsdon. The Carews had established a dynasty at Beddington in the 14th century. Nicholas was brought up at Court and was a constant companion of Henry VIII from before the time when Henry became King. He is said to have answered Henry rather unwisely during a game of bowls, incurring the King's displeasure. More seriously he was accused of being implicated in a plot with certain others at Court and accused of treason. He was taken to the Tower and executed on 3 March 1539.

Ben Clapp – Lived at 40 Warwick Road in the 1920s. He was chief development engineer to John Logie Baird and between them they were developing television using medium-wave radio frequencies, as opposed to the UHF that carries the pictures and sound on today's system. Clapp had a workshop and basic studio at his home, together with a transmitting mast some 250 feet high. In 1928 Baird manned the Coulsdon studio and transmitted a moving picture by radio to New York, where Clapp was demonstrating the system to the press, the first transatlantic television hook-up in the world.

Nicholas Carew
Courtesy of London Borough of Sutton Heritage Service

Colegrime (Colgrym) – This was a Coulsdon family in the 14th and 15th centuries, one of whom, **John**, left his mark on English Law in 1328 by demanding the use of 'Borough English' – the succession to his property by his youngest son, a custom among villeins – rather than the gentry's system of primogeniture *(inheritance by frist-born)*. Another Colegrime, **Robert,** achieved a reversion to primogeniture 11 years later. Following the 1381 Peasants' Revolt, **Charles** illegally enclosed a patch of common wasteland, his brother **Walter** killed a neighbour's sow and, more seriously, kept a boar which he egged on to kill the lord's boar. The varied escapades of two sons and three daughters of John can be followed in the court rolls until 1446. The 1762 Messeder field map of Coulsdon shows two 'Colegrime' farms, and until early in the 20th century 'Plumtree Cottage' in Coulsdon Road was known as 'Colegrimes' Cottages'. There is still a house of this name on Bradmore Green.

Captain William Coombes – William went to sea at an early age and did so well that he was given the mastership of a brig *The Sally* in 1759 trading between London and Charlestown in South Carolina. In 1762 he was given command of a ship named *America* armed against privateers. Though still successfully plying his trade on the oceans, in 1779 he took the tenancy of Welcomes Farm – now Kenley – living there between voyages and becoming a member of the jury of the Court Leet. He retired from the sea in 1783, becoming a full-time sheep farmer for the last seven years of his life. He is buried at St John's.

PERSONALITIES

Andrew Crawford (1825-1926) – centenarian – was a Scot and the father of Revd J C Crawford, the chaplain of Cane Hill Asylum. When his son was obliged to leave the hospital and resign his local councillorship in 1919, they moved to Merton but returned to Coulsdon the following year to vote in the elections for the Coulsdon & Purley UDC. Andrew was then 96 and retained his faculties to the end, recalling the Reform Bill being passed and the Corn Exchange riots.

Revd John Charles Crawford (1849-1935) – was the first chaplain of Cane Hill Asylum in 1883 where he served for 36 years before being obliged to retire in 1919, aged 70. He was chairman of Coulsdon Parish Council and arranged many musical concerts locally for good causes. He had been a first-class cricketer for Kent and made the Cane Hill team one of the strongest in the area. His three sons were all famous cricketers.

John Neville Crawford

John Neville Crawford (1886-1963) – son of the above, was born at Cane Hill and achieved great fame as an all-round cricketer for Repton School and Surrey before becoming the youngest man to play for England. He enjoyed success in the test matches in Australia in 1907-1908 and later represented South Australia before resuming his Surrey career in 1919. He still holds the record for the highest score by an Englishman abroad, 354.

Crufts – The world famous dog show of this name started in 1891, when its founder, Charles Cruft, who had been a traveller for Spratt's Dog Biscuits, started the show as his own very successful business. Interestingly, he never owned a dog! The show retained the Cruft name after it was purchased in 1942 by the Kennel Club. Charles Cruft died in 1938 and his grandson Charles Edward Cruft moved to Coulsdon in 1946 from Sevenoaks, starting the kennelling business at Windmill Farm which he ran until 1976. The business in Stites Hill Road is currently owned by Jonathan and Jane Risley. Charles Edward Cruft died in 1999 at his retirement home in Ottery St Mary, Devon.

Ian Currie – 'Weatherman' Ian Currie moved to Coulsdon from Wallington in 1979. A graduate in geography and earth science, he was a teacher for 20 years. He is a fellow of the Royal Meteorological Society, has written many weather books and writes a number of weekly weather columns in local newspapers. He is a weather consultant to insurance companies, local firms and hospital trusts. He has appeared in and on the national media many times.

Canon Henry Granville Dickson – He was rector of St John's in Coulsdon from 1896 to 1929. Before moving to the Bradmore Green rectory when it was built in 1915, he lived in 'St Ruan', a large house at the junction of Hayes Lane and Abbots Lane – now in Kenley. He preached the gospel not only in St John's but also at the mission halls in Brighton Road, St Peter's Hall in Hayes Lane, Little Roke and Old Lodge Lane. He walked every foot of the way between these until he was well past 80, using the many field paths when necessary. The route that took him to and from St John's is called Canon's Hill in his memory.

(Right):

Cllr F H B Ellis

F H B Ellis – Ellis lived in 'Pound Cottage' on Coulsdon Road and represented the community on Coulsdon & Purley UDC as a councillor and twice as the Chairman of

**Sir William E Goodenough, GCB at
entrance to Parsons Pightle 1934**

Note galleon on gate pillar

Courtesy of Purley Library

Lady Margaret Goodenough

Hon. Thomas Harley

A drawing by E F Bishop

Brian Hope-Taylor

Photograph courtesy of Hulton Picture Library

the Council. An enthusiastic photographer, he recorded the development of Old Coulsdon in the 1920s and 1930s. Many of his photographs are held by Croydon Libraries. He died in 1945.

Admiral Sir William Goodenough – Born at Portsmouth in 1867, he was Commodore of a light cruiser squadron - flying his flag on HMS *Southampton* – at the battles of Heligoland Bight, the Dogger Bank and the battle of Jutland during World War I. His tattered ensign now hangs in St John's Church. On retiring from the Navy after 50 years' distinguished service, during which he was awarded a number of honours including the Order of the Rising Sun of Japan, the French Croix de Guerre and was later appointed Knight Grand Cross of the Most Noble Order of the Bath, he lived at Parson's Pightle. He served for three years as President of the Royal Geographical Society, an organization that had been founded by one of his ancestors.

Lady Margaret Goodenough – She was the eldest daughter of 4th Lord Sheffield of Horsted Keynes. She founded the Old Coulsdon Women's Institute in 1932, provided a meeting place by furnishing stables at Parson's Pightle, and was President. She was Divisional Commissioner for the Girl Guides in the 1920s; on formation of Old Coulsdon District in 1950 she became President until her death in 1956.

Cecilia Goodenough (1905-1998) – Born in Dartmouth, she was the second daughter of Admiral and Lady Goodenough. She grew up in South Africa and was awarded a degree in history at Oxford in 1927. Following her father's death she lived with her mother at Parson's Pightle and became involved in many aspects of the work of the Church of England in Southwark Diocese.

Hon. Thomas Harley – He took over the tenancy of Hooley House in 1760 after the death of his father-in-law, Edward Bangham, MP for Leominster. He was the 4th son of the 3rd Earl of Oxford, and became Lord Mayor of London in 1767 and later a Member of Parliament as well as a banker of distinction in the City. He was one of Coulsdon's more eminent citizens and left a lasting landmark by planting the folly of beech trees on the crown of Farthing Downs. Only one of the original seven trees exists.

Brian Hope-Taylor – lived with his parents near Purley Oaks in the 1940s. After serving in the RAF he became a free-lance artist of considerable merit, before turning to freelance archaeology. His archaeological work on Farthing Downs in 1948 is written in Surrey Archaeological Society's journal Vol.50. He did a variety of rescue digs in Surrey, excavated the Iron Age fort at War Coppice and carried out the first British excavation on a motte at Abinger. He was involved in the early days of work on York Minster. He has lived in Cambridge for many years.

Frederick George Kerswell JP (1883-1953) – He was a retired linen merchant, starting as an apprentice and eventually founding his own business. He served on Coulsdon & Purley UDC from 1938 until his death and was chairman from 1942 to 1945. He was involved with wartime civil defence and is said to have visited every air-raid incident in the district. Before he died he gave up some of his activities but was still a member of over 100 committees and public bodies. He was made an alderman by Surrey County Council, representing Coulsdon division from 1946 until 1953.

The unveiling of the memorial clock at Marlpit Lane recreation ground 1957 in memory of Cllr F G Kerswell JP

Frank Lazenby – He was born in Liverpool in 1901 and began his career as a journalist in Hitchin. After World War I he came to work for *The Croydon Advertiser*. His talent as an artist was apparent at an early age and while working for the *Advertiser* he doubled as a sports' cartoonist and later became a freelance artist and cartoonist. His wife, Doris (née Hoare) came from an Old Coulsdon farming family. They moved into Old Coulsdon from Purley in 1962. Frank Lazenby was an active member of *The Bourne Society* and frequently gave talks on the history of the district.

Charles Leisten (1824-1925) – centenarian – came to Coulsdon in 1903, two years after two of his sons had set up a stationer's and newsagent's shop opposite *The Red Lion*. One of them, Ernest, was killed during World War I, but three sons and a widow mourned the passing of the centenarian, who was buried at Bandon Hill.

George Leppard (1843-1903) – was born at Avin's Farm, Ardingly but came to Coulsdon in 1869. He took Hartley Farm in 1872, where he remained until his death. He was for many years an overseer and a churchwarden. The mourners at his funeral included Edmund Byron.

Stanley Littlechild – moved to Old Coulsdon with his wife in 1933 and from 1939 became an elected local government member. Eventually he was elected Mayor of Croydon and was the longest serving local councillor. His wife, Kate, was head of her own school and a chairman of Old Coulsdon Residents' Association. The couple lived for many years at the former nurses' home, 536 Coulsdon Road. Councillor Littlechild died in 1997.

Sir Douglas Lovelock, KCB – Born in London, Sir Douglas and Lady Valerie have lived in 'The Old House' in Coulsdon Road, for the past 30 years. A Civil Servant all his working life, he rose to be chairman of HM Customs and Excise from 1977 until 1983. Following his retirement from the Service, he was appointed First Church Estates Commissioner, responsible for all the church of England's investments in property and business, retiring in 1993 when he was 70. He has been Chairman of the Whitgift Foundation since 1994. He was founder and organiser of the Development fund at St John's Church, raising some £164,000.

Harriet Markham, née Burdett (1848-1887) – was born in Bloomsbury and taught at "Riddlesdown School for infants and older pupils" from 1877 until her death. The school averaged 111 pupils and was continually involved in change, with the threat of closure and movement to a new building. Harriet was teaching, training a pupil teacher, and bringing up her own nine children. Her gravestone reads "She was called to her rest after a short illness induced by mental anxiety for their (her school-children) spiritual welfare and that of her school".

Cllr S E Littlechild
Courtesy of London Borough of Croydon

Doris E Martin – Miss Martin founded Downland School for pupils 4-11 years old and administered it very successfully until 1962. She was the youngest of five children and having trained to be a children's nanny, she worked for a number of years in America. In 1932 she lived in 'Pound Cottage', 202 Coulsdon Road. A much loved local lady, she died in 1993.

Bertram E Mitchell – was headmaster at Purley County Grammar School for Boys from 1920 to 1945. He is remembered for his strict discipline, a tradition upheld by subsequent headmasters, **Dr H Birchall** (1945-1966) and **D G S Akers** (1969-1988) *(qv)*.

PERSONALITIES

Dr James Matthew Moody (died 1915) – was medical superintendent of Cane Hill Asylum from 1883 until his death. He was a son of John Moody, Fleet Surgeon RN of Great Warley, Essex and a student of St Thomas' Hospital. He participated in the musical concerts at Cane Hill and was later knighted for his services to medicine.

Oscar Wilson Moorsom-Roberts – was the owner of Hooley House and farm during the latter part of the 19th century. He took the additional name Moorsom when he married Mary Hasted Moorsom in 1884. Around 1900 he began building cottages for his tenants facing Farthing Downs and these are the current houses numbered 26-48 Downs Road. Always an eccentric, Moorsom-Roberts renamed Hooley House 'St Chad's Court' and is said at one time to have dressed all his male staff in kilts.

John Cunliffe Pickersgill-Cunliffe (sen.) (1819-1873) – was the son of John Pickersgill of Netherne House and took the additional name of Cunliffe on inheriting the property of an aunt in Yorkshire. He lived at Hooley House and was a merchant and banker in London, being head of the influential American banking firm of John Pickersgill & Sons. He was elected MP for Bewdley on a casual vacancy in 1869 but his election was set aside and voided on petition. He retired with a large fortune but was unfortunately killed crossing the railway line at Purley station. He died in Guy's Hospital and is buried in St John's, along with his son of the same names.

Gordon Pirie   1958

Gordon Pirie (1931-1991) – The family moved to Coulsdon from Yorkshire and Gordon was educated at Purley County School for Boys. He rose from being a bank clerk to an athlete by way of an unusually severe training programme. He was often to be seen running over Farthing Downs wearing army boots. In 1953 Pirie broke the world six mile record and captured six other British records. He ran the mile in under four minutes. In 1956 he took the 5,000m world record and three days later shattered the 3,000m world record. In the 1970s his family moved to New Zealand, returning in the 1980s. It is estimated that he covered a total of over 200,000 miles afoot.

Thomas Rivers (1879-1967) – was the last of a family of wheelwrights that lived on Coulsdon Common. His father, also Thomas, was one of eight sons of the founder of the business on that site – all of whom became wheelwrights. Another of the eight sons was John Rivers who founded a wheelwright's and blacksmith's business in Caterham Valley in 1871, a firm which was carried on by his

(Right): **The Wheelwright's Cottages, Coulsdon Common**

2000

grandsons as a motor body and lawn mower engineering business. The wheelwright's shop on Coulsdon Common closed in about 1952, but the adjacent family cottages survive in Stites Hill Road. The family assisted in repairs to the nearby windmills.

Revd David Dale Stewart (1817-1900) – was Rector of Coulsdon from 1878 to 1896 having previously (from 1857) been rector of St Peter's, South Croydon. He wrote *A Summary of the Psalms* and died at Pebble Hill Cottage, Limpsfield. He is buried in St Peter's, Limpsfield.

Walter Stride (1840-1899) – of The Grange was the first chairman of Coulsdon & District Parish Council in 1895. He lived in Coulsdon for 12 years and was chairman of the South American Railway Companies, director of Cannock Chase Colliery Company, and of J C & J Field Ltd of Lambeth. He was president of Coulsdon Cricket Club and Coulsdon Conservative Association, as well as being a churchwarden and a mason.

John & William Toller – appear regularly in the Coulsdon court rolls between 1385 and 1415 for offences such as arranging a daughter's marriage without the lord's permission and for not maintaining their house. This lack of maintenance led to the surrender of Tollers to the lord, and the estate was subsequently let on lease. William died without leaving any beast to meet the lord's claim for a heriot. William's son, Walter, was reported to have fled without payment of a chevage tax and – in 1437 – William junior committed the same offence when he fled to Kent where he was in the custody of his mother, Isable.

Joseph Tucker – was the last private owner of Portnalls. In 1873 he diverted Portnalls Road to its present line from another further east, and laid out roads on the line of former footpaths at Hollyme Oak and Rickman Hill. In 1907 he commenced the laying out of roads adjoining Cane Hill for bungalows and villas. The present Portnalls House was built in 1880 but a massive barn belonging to its predecessor was demolished in 1939. A daughter took some important early photographs of the district.

John Tutt – in 1872 worked the Coulsdon windmill opposite Windmill Cottage for Albert Gilbert. Soon afterwards when Gilbert moved his bakery business to Purley, Tutt carried on by himself for a couple of years before handing over to his father, George, and to his brother, Alexander. They worked both mills until the second one stopped working in 1893, receiving occasional assistance from another brother, William, who assisted with the stone-dressing.

Robert Webb (1815-1891) – was the son of Colonel Byron's coachman and the Coulsdon schoolmistress who served for 40 years. He was employed by Edmund Byron until 1884 and died in the house where he was born. Greatly respected, he was described as a steadfast and quiet man.

THE BOURNE SOCIETY

The Bourne Society was founded in 1956 and takes its name from the underground streams which follow the lines of the A22 and A23 roads, meeting in Purley to flow northwards and join the River Wandle, which flows into the Thames at Wandsworth.

The objects of the Society – England's largest local history society – are to extend the knowledge of local history in Caterham, Chaldon, Chelsham, Chipstead, Coulsdon, Farleigh, Godstone, Kenley, Purley, Sanderstead, Whyteleafe, Warlingham and Woldingham, and to ensure the preservation of records and objects of historical interest. The Society's Membership Secretary, Mrs. J. Emery, 118 Coulsdon Road, Coulsdon, Surrey CR5 2LB, will be happy to provide details of membership and subscription rates. The Society's telephone number is 01883 349287.

The Bourne Society is a registered charity, and as well as general work it has active special-interest groups in archaeology, industrial archaeology, landscape history, photography and pub history. Regular meetings, events and outings are arranged. A wide range of publications are produced, including a quarterly **Bulletin** and annual *Local History Records* which are sent free to members. For prices and current availability contact John Tyerman, Publications Co-ordinator, 60 Onslow Gardens, Sanderstead CR2 9AT, telephone 020 8657 1202.

Some recent publications —

Books:

Village History Series. Vol. 1–Purley, editor Andy Higham (1996); Vol. 2–Caterham, editor Gwyneth Fookes (1997); Vol. 3–Sanderstead, editor Joy Gadsby (1998); Vol. 4–Warlingham, editor Dorothy Tutt (1999); Vol. 5–Coulsdon, editor Ian Scales (2000); Vol. 6–Chaldon in preparation for publication in 2001; Vol. 7–Kenley in preparation.

A Centenary History of the Chipstead Valley Railway (Tattenham Corner Branch Line, 1897-1997)

The Way We Were - A Bourne Society Book of Days by John D. Matthews

A Surrey Childhood in the 1930s and 1940s by Muriel Neal

Leaflets:

Getting to know our Downland Villages – No. 1. Sanderstead (1997); No. 2. Godstone (1998)

Postcards:

Ancient and modern views of places in the Bourne Society area are available from local stationers.